Contents

**OFFICE FOR STANDARDS
IN EDUCATION**

Inspecting School Sixth Forms

Supplement to the *Handbook for Inspecting Secondary Schools*

This supplement contains new requirements and guidance
Effective from September 2001

HMI 325

London: The Stationery Office

Inspection Quality Division
Office for Standards in Education
Alexandra House
33 Kingsway
London WC2B 6SE

Telephone: 020 7421 6800

Website: www.ofsted.gov.uk

Introduction

The government's White Paper *Learning to Succeed: A New Framework for Post-16 Learning (1999)* set out the intention that sixth forms in schools should be inspected in as much depth as other school provision and 16–19 provision elsewhere. The new requirements and guidance in this *Supplement* are intended to strengthen the inspection of school sixth forms.

The Learning and Skills Act 2000 extended the remit of the Office for Standards in Education (OFSTED) to include the inspection of all 16–19 education in, for example, sixth form and other further education colleges, from April 2001. The Adult Learning Inspectorate (ALI) is responsible for the inspection of all work-based learning and adult education. Most inspections of colleges are joint inspections involving OFSTED and the ALI. Her Majesty's Inspectors (HMI) and inspectors from the ALI, with additional inspectors appointed by OFSTED and the ALI carry out these inspections.

The *Common Inspection Framework* (March 2001) applies to the inspection of colleges and training providers. School sixth-form inspections continue to be carried out under section 10 of the School Inspections Act 1996. They are not subject to the same Framework directly. However, the arrangements in this *Supplement* bring the inspection of school sixth forms and colleges as much into line as possible.

The Learning and Skills Act (Schedule 7) makes a specific requirement relating to the inspection of schools. It relates to the adequacy of provision in sixth forms. Where inspectors judge that the sixth form is 'inadequate', this must be reported.

Part 1

Changes in School Sixth Forms

Changes to post-16 qualifications were introduced in September 2000. The aims were to:

- provide a range of qualifications from which students can choose and gain credit;
- ensure that qualifications are worthwhile and valued, and enable students to combine academic and vocational studies coherently;
- offer scope for students to broaden their knowledge, understanding and skills but also, at the same time, to advance their studies through specialisation;
- promote the achievement of high levels of key skills;
- offer clear progression routes into higher education, employment and further training.

The Qualifications and Curriculum Authority (QCA) has recently published guidance on managing Curriculum 2000 for 16–19 students.[1]

National Qualifications Framework

The National Qualifications Framework has six levels. It is designed to ensure broad equivalence across different types of qualifications. The courses and qualifications most likely to be found in school sixth forms are shaded in table 1.

Table 1. National Qualifications Framework levels

Level	General	Vocationally related	Occupational
5	Higher level qualifications		Level 5 NVQ
4	First degree, foundation degree Higher National Diploma (HND) Higher National Certificate (HNC)		Level 4 NVQ
3: Advanced level	GCE A level, including AS and AE awards	AVCE 3–, 6–, and 12–unit	Level 3 NVQ
2: Intermediate level	GCSE grades A*–C	Intermediate GNVQ	Level 2 NVQ
1: Foundation level	GCSE grades D–G	Foundation GNVQ	Level 1 NVQ
Entry level	Certificate of (educational) achievement		

General qualifications are in specific subjects. Vocationally related qualifications give a broad introduction to vocational areas. Occupational qualifications link into specific jobs.

---

[1]   *Managing Curriculum 2000 for 16-19 Students* is available on the QCA website at **www.qca.org.uk**

GCE AS and A levels and advanced extension awards (AEA)

All advanced subsidiary (AS) and A-level subjects had new specifications in 2000. They are modular, and six units are normally required to complete an A-level qualification. Three units, usually studied in the first year work of a two-year A-level course, lead to the AS qualification. AS units are assessed and graded to match the standards expected from students who are halfway through an advanced course of study. AS, and a further three units, referred to as A2 and normally taken in the second year of study, make up the A-level course.

AS courses are intended to increase the range of subjects that students study in their first year in the sixth form. The number will vary between schools and for individual students. Students might take four or five AS subjects, and then continue with three to A level. An AS programme might be combined with a vocationally related course.

The Advanced Extension Award (AEA) is being introduced in summer 2002. The award is intended to stretch the most able A-level students to greater depths of understanding and critical thinking than required at A level, and differentiate between the most able candidates who would typically gain grade A. The award will be at merit and distinction levels, but will not be available in all subjects.

Vocationally related courses

GNVQ courses also have new specifications. Advanced GNVQ is now the advanced vocational certificate of education (AVCE).

A double-award AVCE consists of 12 units; 8 are usually mandatory and a further 4 are optional. The award is equivalent to two A levels, with double grades AA to EE. In addition to the double-award AVCE, 6-unit and 3-unit vocational A levels are available, corresponding to single GCE A and AS levels, respectively. The 3-unit qualification is only available in four areas: business, engineering, ICT, and health and social care.

Intermediate and foundation GNVQs consist of 6 units. They have new specifications but are more similar to the courses that preceded them than AVCE. They are graded as pass, merit and distinction.

Further information about vocational qualifications, the assessment arrangements and their equivalence to GCSE and AS/A level accreditation is included in *Curriculum 2000 – Implementing the Changes to 16–19 Qualifications* (QCA, 1999).

Key Skills

It is hoped that sixth-form students will work towards qualifications in key skills. There are three main key skills:

- application of number;
- communication;
- information technology.

Three wider key skills are:

- working with others;
- improving own learning and performance (study skills);
- problem-solving.

All GCE AS/A level and AVCE specifications identify opportunities for students to produce evidence of their attainment in key skills.

Individual key skills can be certificated at five levels. Level 3 is appropriate for supporting work in AS, A-level and advanced vocational courses. The three main key skills together currently constitute the key skills qualification. Individual key skills will attract 'points' in the Universities and Colleges Admissions System (UCAS) (see below).

In the main key skills, students are assessed on a portfolio of evidence which may include:

- work from the range of courses being followed;
- work done as part of enrichment or extra-curricular activities, or outside school; or
- work done specially for the key-skills qualification.

In addition, for each unit, there is an externally set and marked test. There are exemptions for students taking some English, mathematics or computing/ICT qualifications. Some qualifications exempt students only from the test, while others give total exemption.

Schools choose whether or not to offer the qualifications or teach to the key skills specifications; they are not compulsory in the post-16 curriculum. Key skills 'elements' are no longer mandatory in GNVQ or AVCE qualifications although many schools will probably still seek to cover the key-skills requirements in vocational courses. Key-skills specifications are available from QCA.[2]

Awarding bodies

The former GCE examination boards and vocational awarding bodies for England have merged to form three new awarding bodies:

- Assessment and Qualifications Alliance (AQA): **www.aqa.org.uk**
- Edexcel: **www.edexcel.org.uk**
- Oxford Cambridge and RSA Examinations (OCR): **www.ocr.org.uk**

Specifications for GCE AS and A levels, GNVQs and AVCEs can be obtained from these bodies, or downloaded from their websites.

---

2   QCA Publications, PO Box 99, Sudbury, Suffolk, CO10 6SN. Tel: 01787 884444. Fax: 01787 312950. The specifications are also available on the Internet at **www.qca.org.uk**

UCAS points tariff from 2002

UCAS is introducing a new tariff system from September 2002. It embraces vocational qualifications and key skills.

The tariff system is:

Points	7	10	13	17	20	28	30	35	38	40	42	48	50	60	72	80	100	120	160	200	240
A/AS, AVCE & GNVQ																					
1-unit	E	D	C	B	A																
3-unit (AS)				E		D				C			B	A							
6-unit (A)										E				D		C	B	A			
12-unit (AVCE)																E		D	C	B	A
Key skills units																					
key skill level		2			3	4															

Quality of post-16 provision and funding arrangements

The Learning and Skills Council (LSC), through local LSCs, is responsible for the quality and funding of post-16 education and training, but the LSCs will not directly monitor sixth-form provision. Funding for sixth forms from the LSC will begin in April 2002, but it will be routed to schools through local education authorities (LEAs).

The Learning and Skills Act requires that a copy of the report and summary following the inspection of schools with a sixth form is sent to the LSC.

Part 2

Requirements for Inspecting School Sixth Forms

From September 2001, sixth forms will feature more strongly in school inspection and reporting. The main changes are that:

- **full and short inspections attract more inspector days** to allow inspection teams to evaluate thoroughly the quality and standards in the sixth form and its cost-effectiveness;
- a **modified inspection** *Schedule* is used in the sixth form;
- **sixth forms of a given size have similar coverage and depth of inspection** irrespective of whether the school is selected for a full or short inspection;
- **inspectors must be 'endorsed'** to lead and report on subjects and courses inspected in detail in the sixth form;
- schools will be invited to use a **student's questionnaire** to seek students' views about the sixth form;
- reports will include a sixth-form annex to the summary and a section on sixth-form subjects and courses;
- inspection teams report formally where they judge a school to have an **inadequate sixth form;**
- **additional summary judgements** are included in the inspector's Notebook and the Record of Corporate Judgements (RCJ); Notebooks will be used for sixth-form subjects in short inspections;
- inspection teams make summative judgements about the **quality of provision in subjects and courses** that are inspected, and the **effectiveness of leadership and management** as they affect the sixth form;
- a copy of the inspection report and summary must be sent to the LSC.

Despite the emphasis on the sixth form, inspection teams should continue to **inspect and report on the school as a whole,** paying attention to issues of equal opportunities and educational inclusion.[3] The **principle of differentiated inspection** also remains. In full and short inspections, the inspection of Key Stages 3 and 4 should be unaffected.

---

3 See *Evaluating Educational Inclusion* (OFSTED, 2000). This publication is available on OFSTED's website at **www.ofsted.gov.uk**

Enhancement of inspection teams

The extra time added to the inspections of schools with sixth forms depends mainly on the size of the sixth form. Table 2 gives a rough guide of the additional days and the time the inspection team should spend inspecting the sixth form.

Table 2: Enhancement of inspections

Sixth-form size	Extra time: full inspections (inspector days)	Extra time: short inspections (inspector days)	Sixth-form inspection time (inspector days)
20–100	+4–5	+6	9
101–200	+8–9	+12	15
201–300	+11–12	+18	21
300+	+14–15	+22	25

For example, for a school with 980 pupils including 160 in the sixth form:

- a full inspection is allocated about 59 days compared with 51 days prior to September 2001;
- a short inspection is allocated about 25 days compared with 13 days.

Normally, no extra time is given to inspections where the sixth form has fewer than 20 students.

Inspection requirements

In the **sixth form**, the inspection team must:

- use the modified *Schedule* in Part 4 of this *Supplement* in both full and short inspections;
- sample work across the range of provision as fully as possible, interpreting performance data and evaluating the quality of teaching and learning;
- inspect a cross-section of subjects or courses in detail, selected on the basis of a set of principles;

In **Key Stages 3 and 4**, the inspection team must:

- continue to use the *Schedule* in the *Handbook for Inspecting Secondary Schools*.

Modified Schedule

The modified *Schedule* to be used in sixth forms adapts the section 10 *Schedule* to align it with the *Common Inspection Framework* used in colleges.

The modifications emphasise:

- the experiences and achievements of individual students, and in particular:
  - the suitability of the courses and programmes to students' prior attainment, potential and aspirations;
  - their personal development, attitudes and skills, including how well they are prepared for work and further study beyond school;
  - the guidance and support of students before they embark on courses, during their studies and in moving on from school;
- the views of students about the sixth form;
- how leadership and management affect the sixth form.

Table 3 summarises the main changes to different sections of the *Schedule*. Part 4 of this *Supplement* gives guidance on interpreting the evaluation requirements and criteria in the sixth form.

Table 3: Summary of modifications to the section 10 Schedule for sixth-form inspection

1. What sort of school is it?	• includes a requirement to report where a school has an inadequate sixth form; • includes an annex to the summary to report on the effectiveness of the sixth form, standards and quality in subjects and courses, and students' views.
2. How high are standards? 2.1 The school's results and achievements	• reinforces the use of value-added data and information about retention of students on courses; • includes evaluation of standards in key skills; • includes progression to further and higher education or employment.
2. How high are standards? 2.2 Students' attitudes, values and personal development	• includes how well students develop the attitudes and skills to prepare them for further study or work.
3. How well are students taught?	• includes the quality of teaching of key skills where these are taught; • recognises that in the sixth form there may be increased emphasis on independent study.
4. How good are the curricular and other opportunities?	• emphasises the match of courses and programmes with individual needs; • includes evaluation of enrichment programmes; • recognises that provision may be in collaboration with other schools and colleges, and should respond to local circumstances.
5. How well does the school care for its students?	• emphasises the guidance of students onto and through courses; • includes careers guidance; • includes identification of and provision for individual needs; • emphasises assessment.
6. How well does the school work in partnership with parents?	• incorporates students' views of the sixth form.
7. How well is the school led and managed?	• focuses on the effect of leadership and management on the sixth form, including quality assurance and ensuring cost-effectiveness; • includes the availability and use of resources in the sixth form.
8. What should the school do to improve further?	• includes specific issues that relate to the sixth form.
10. The standards and quality of teaching in subjects and courses	• includes the evaluation of work sampled across the sixth-form curriculum and subjects or courses inspected in detail; • a separate section on sixth-form subjects and courses is included in the inspection report.

Subjects and courses

The inspection team will:

- sample work as widely as possible across the range of the school's sixth-form provision;
- inspect some subjects and courses in more detail.

You must follow up any strengths or weaknesses in the sixth-form provision so that you represent the school fairly and accurately. Table 4 gives the approximate number of subjects or courses inspected in detail.

Table 4: Numbers of subjects inspected in detail

Size of sixth form	Number of subjects inspected in detail
20–100	5
101–200	9
201–300	13
300+	15

In very small sixth forms with fewer than 20 students, look at all the courses offered.

Subjects and courses usually found in schools are grouped into curriculum areas shown in table 5. Similar and additional areas are used in college inspections. Using the principles set out below, inspection contractors and registered inspectors should select the cross-section of subjects and courses to be inspected in detail.

- **English, mathematics and a science subject** should always be included.
- Other subjects should be drawn from across **as many curriculum areas** as possible. Where possible a modern foreign language should be included in addition to English from the 'English, languages and communications' area.
- **Subjects that appear from pre-inspection data to be particularly weak must be inspected.**
- **Vocationally related courses** should be duly represented.
- Courses at **different levels** should be inspected. Where a subject or course is offered at two levels, for example advanced and intermediate vocational courses, standards and quality at both levels should be evaluated.
- Where a school is part of a **shared sixth form,** the subjects inspected in detail should be in that school where possible, with sampling in other schools. Circumstances may dictate more inspection outside the inspected school. Where substantial provision is made outside the school, this should be inspected to test the effectiveness of the management decisions to provide for the sixth form in this way.
- In **small sixth forms** (up to 100), attention should be given mainly to the subjects or courses followed by most students, but English, mathematics and a science should be inspected where possible.

Choice will depend on factors such as the **emphasis of the school's provision, the strengths and weaknesses, inspection expertise available** in the inspection team, **and take-up by students.** Normally, a subject will not be inspected in detail if it has fewer than five students.

Endorsement of inspectors for sixth-form inspection

Evaluating sixth-form subjects rigorously needs inspectors who are expert in the subjects and courses they inspect. Keep up to date with the specifications for the subjects or courses you inspect and other changes that affect sixth forms.

From September 2001, you can only **lead and report** on the standards and quality in **individual subjects or courses** if, in addition to being on the roll of inspectors, you have the relevant post-16 endorsements. Other inspectors qualified for the secondary phase, and lay inspectors, can contribute to inspection across the sixth form. Queries about endorsement should be raised with OFSTED's Assistant Registrar (telephone: 020 7421 6794).

Equal opportunities and educational inclusion

All inspectors share the responsibility for determining whether a school, including its sixth form, is effective for all its students, whatever their educational needs or personal circumstances. This requires a good understanding of:

- the characteristics of the school and its students;
- the recruitment patterns and retention rates to programmes and courses for different groups of students;
- whether individual goals and targets for students are appropriate and they are making as much progress towards meeting them as they can;
- how students' different needs and aspirations are being met.

You should be aware of the responsibilities and duties of schools regarding equal opportunities, particularly relating to discrimination of grounds of gender, race and disability.[4]

The legislation included in the footnote underpin national policies on inclusion, on maximising achievement, and on the important role schools have in fostering better personal, community and race relations, and in dealing with, as well as preventing, racism and promoting race equality.[5]

Student's questionnaire

The questionnaire included in annex A is to seek the views of students about the sixth form. Schools should be invited to use it, but its use by the school and completion by students are voluntary. Annex A also includes notes for the school.

Where the questionnaire is used, the responses of individual students must be **confidential** to the inspection team, but you should share any significant general issues with the school.

Use the responses to the questionnaires, together with evidence from your discussions with students to capture what students value and what they feel should be improved in the sixth form. A digest of their views together with the inspection team's response to them is included in the sixth-form annex to the summary report.

---

4   Sex Discrimination Act 1975; Disability Discrimination Act 1995; Race Relations Act 1976 and the Race Relations (Amendment) Act 2000; Special Educational Needs and Disability Act 2001.

5   See annex: 'Issues for Inspection arising from the Stephen Lawrence Inquiry' (Macpherson Report) in *Evaluating Educational Inclusion* (OFSTED, 2000) p.33.

Table 5: Curriculum areas

Curriculum area	Level 3 Courses GCE A and AS; AVCEs	Level 2 Courses GNVQ(I), GCSE	Level 1 Courses GNVQ(F)
Mathematics and Sciences	Mathematics Chemistry Biology Physics Science Geology Electronics Science V	Science V	Science V
Engineering, design and manufacturing	Design and technology Food technology Engineering V Manufacturing V	Manufacturing V Engineering V	Engineering V Manufacturing V
Business	Business studies Economics Business V	Business V	Business V
ICT	Computing ICT ICT V	ICT V	ICT V
Hospitality, sports, leisure and travel	Physical education Leisure and recreation V Hospitality and catering V Travel and tourism V	Leisure and tourism V Hospitality and catering V	Leisure and tourism V Hospitality and catering V
Health and social care	Health and social care V	Health and social care V	Health and social care V
Visual and performing arts and media	Art Art and Design V Music Music technology Dance Drama and theatre studies Film studies Performing arts V Media Studies Media V	Art and Design V Performing Arts V Media V	Art and Design V Performing Arts V
Humanities	Classical civilisation Latin Classical Greek Geography History Religious studies Government and politics Law Sociology Psychology Philosophy		
English, languages and communication	English Communication studies Modern languages		

GCSE courses (Level 2), particularly English and mathematics, may be offered in the sixth form. In the table 'V' signifies vocational courses such as AVCE and GNVQ intermediate or foundation courses. In a minority of schools, other vocational courses might include, for example, agriculture.

Enhanced full and short inspections

The deployment of inspectors and the organisation of inspections are matters for the contractor and the registered inspector, but the following principles will normally apply.

Full inspections

- Some or all inspectors are given more time to enable them to focus more on the sixth form.
- Specialist inspectors may join the team for one or more days to inspect subjects in the sixth form.
- The school is given feedback on sixth-form subjects as well as subjects in Key Stages 3 and 4.

Short inspections

- The inspection of Key Stages 3 and 4 of the school should be the same as for a school without a sixth form.
- The overall approach is that of any short inspection, with a sharp focus on the overall strengths and areas for improvement in the school, but with a particular emphasis on the sixth form.
- A 'core' team of inspectors will be responsible for the short inspection element and inspection of Key Stages 3 and 4.
- Members of the 'core' team will usually also inspect some sixth form subjects.
- Specialist inspectors join for one or more days to inspect subjects in the sixth form and contribute to the sampling of sixth-form provision.
- Subject or course feedback is only given on sixth-form provision since the inspection at Key Stages 3 and 4 is not subject-focused.

Full and short inspections must be completed within 10 working days. Most inspections will be completed within a single week, but some could span two weeks to accommodate the inspection of particular sixth-form subjects. Where this happens, the inspection of these subjects should precede the main part of the inspection. Hold to the principle that all first-hand evidence must be gathered before the final team meeting.

Inspection reports

Changes to the report structure are to ensure that the evaluation of sixth forms is prominent. They also allow a 'sixth-form report' to be extracted.

Inspection contractors should send a copy of the inspection report and summary of a school with a sixth form to the LSC.

The **outline structures of full and short inspection reports are shown below**. New sections are in dashed boxes, and other new features are in italics.

Full inspection report

Part A. Summary of the report

Summary relating to the whole school

Sixth form annex, summarising:
- *the effectiveness of the sixth form, including overall judgements in each subject inspected and of leadership and management as it affects the sixth form;*
- *support and guidance of students and their views of the sixth form.*

Part B. Commentary

A commentary on the findings in relation to each of the key questions in the *Schedule, including a sub-section within each Schedule section relating to the sixth form.*
A section on 'What should the school do to improve?' *including a subsection relating to the sixth form* where relevant.

Part C. School data and indicators

Data tables *include subsections dealing with the sixth form as a whole*

Part D. Standards and quality of teaching in subjects and courses pre-16

Subject reports, *to Key Stage 4 only.*
Subject reports include a summary of strengths and areas for improvement.

Part E. The standards and quality of teaching in subjects and courses in the sixth form

This part includes:
- *a table of performance data in subjects and courses;*
- *reports on each curriculum area (see Table 5) with:*
  - *brief comments on work sampled;*
  - *specific sections on subjects and courses inspected in detail;*
- *subjects and course reports include:*
  - *a summary of the strengths and areas for improvement;*
  - *an overall judgement about provision.*

Short inspection report

Part A. Summary of the report

Summary relating to the whole school

Sixth form annex, summarising:
- *the effectiveness of the sixth form, including overall judgements in each subject inspected and leadership and management as it affects the sixth form;*
- *support and guidance of students and their views of the sixth form.*

Part B. Commentary

A commentary on each of the issues listed as strengths or areas for improvement for the school as a whole, including brief references to the sixth form where relevant.
A section on 'What should the school do to improve?' *including a subsection relating to the sixth form* where relevant.

Part C. School data and indicators

Data tables *include subsections dealing with the sixth form as a whole.*

Part D. The sixth form

Commentary on the sixth form findings in relation to each of the key questions in the modified Schedule.

Part E. The standards and quality of teaching in subjects and courses in the sixth form

This part includes:
- *a table of performance data in subjects and courses;*
- *reports on each curriculum area (see Table 5) with:*
  - *brief comments on work sampled;*
  - *specific sections on subjects and courses inspected in detail;*
- *subject and course reports include:*
  - *a summary of the strengths and areas for improvement;*
  - *an overall judgement about provision.*

Part 4 of this *Supplement* gives more guidance on how to incorporate sixth-form judgements and evidence relating to each section of the *Schedule* in the report. Examples of the new features of report writing are included in Part 6.

Inadequate sixth forms

The Learning and Skills Act 2000 requires you to report if the school, although it does not require special measures, has an inadequate sixth form. According to schedule 7 of the Act, a school has an inadequate sixth form if:

- 'it is failing or likely to fail to give pupils over compulsory school age an acceptable standard of education'; or if
- 'it has significant weaknesses in one or more areas of its activities for pupils over compulsory school age'.

The Act refers to 'pupils' rather than 'students', but use the term 'students' in the report if this is normally used.

Guidance on making and reporting the judgement and the procedures to be followed are included in Part 5 of this *Supplement*.

Towards the end of the inspection the team must consider whether the sixth form is inadequate.

Amendments to the inspector's Notebook and Record of Corporate Judgements

The inspector's Notebook and the RCJ to be used in the inspection of schools with sixth forms include:

- subsections to record strengths, areas for improvement and overall evaluations of the sixth form;
- additional Judgement Recording Form (JRF) grades;
- in the RCJ, a section for recording the team's judgement about the 'adequacy' of the sixth form.

The new sixth-form JRF grades are of the following kinds:

- those that stem from new criteria or features in the *Schedule* that relate to the sixth form only, such as students' views (RCJ 2.14a);
- those that record judgements about the sixth form where previously only 'school' judgements were required, such as for attendance (RCJ 2F).

In the Notebook from a full inspection, the 'school' judgement should continue to be based on consideration of evidence and judgements relating to all stages, including the sixth form. If a subject is taught only in the sixth form, the 'sixth form' summary judgement and the 'school' judgement will be the same. In the Notebook from a short inspection, the only subject grades recorded in the JRF are for the sixth-form subjects inspected.

Summative judgements about the quality of provision in subjects and courses, and the effectiveness of leadership and management

The annex to the summary report must include summative judgements on:

- the quality of provision in each subject or course inspected in detail;
- leadership and management as they affect the sixth form.

These judgements are also be included in the sixth-form subject and course, and leadership and management sections of the inspection report.

The summative judgements use the **seven-point scale descriptions**: excellent, very good, good, satisfactory, unsatisfactory, poor and very poor. They equate to the five-point scale used for similar summative judgements in colleges as follows.

Sixth form	FE college
Excellent	
Very good	Outstanding
Good	Good
Satisfactory	Satisfactory
Unsatisfactory	Unsatisfactory
Poor	
Very poor	Very weak

Part 4 of the *Supplement* includes guidance on making these summative judgements.

Part 3

Carrying out Enhanced Full and Short Inspections

This part describes what enhanced sixth-form inspection means for schools and the work of registered and team inspectors. It then gives guidance on conducting the inspection.

What it means for the school

The school should see its inspection as a single inspection, not an evaluation in two parts. The registered inspector must ensure that the headteacher, governors and staff are carefully briefed.

In a **full** inspection, the school should notice little difference from its previous inspection, although there will be more inspection of sixth-form lessons.

In a **short** inspection, the school will notice more difference as the sixth form will have more attention than the rest of the school.

In either, schools should not see an enhanced sixth-form inspection as unusual or different. They still receive an inspection which focuses strongly on whole-school issues. The greater focus on the sixth form must not deflect from reporting fairly and accurately on the school as a whole.

What it means for the inspection team

Treat the inspection as a single inspection but with a particular sixth-form focus. The full or short inspection of Key Stages 3 and 4 is the same as in any secondary school and the inspection of the sixth form must be integrated with it.

In **full** inspections:

- there is little difference in the way you gather evidence and make judgements;
- you will simply give more attention to the sixth form than has been the case;
- inspection of some sixth-form subjects may involve specialist inspectors who join the team for this purpose.

In **short** inspections:

- expect to feel differences from previous short inspections;
- the team is likely to consist of those doing the inspection of Key Stages 3 and 4 and contributing to the sixth form, and those who inspect only sixth-form subjects;
- expect differences in team meetings – they need to achieve the right balance between the **short** inspection of the school as a whole, and the inspection of the sixth form. Getting this balance right is critical. Findings about sixth-form subjects need to contribute to, but not dominate, whole-school judgements.

Use the guidance in the *Handbook for Inspecting Secondary Schools* and *Evaluating Educational Inclusion* for inspecting Key Stages 3 and 4.

In some cases, sixth-form provision may be spread across several schools. The focus must remain on the standards and quality of education provided for the students in the school being inspected and the standards they achieve, except where special arrangements are made for inspecting a consortium as a whole.

Planning and carrying out the inspection

☐ Before the inspection

Registered inspector

You need to:

- decide which subjects in the sixth form will be inspected in detail, and which will be sampled (in both **full** and **short** inspections), and give guidance to your team on gathering evidence;

- ensure that the pre-inspection commentary includes distinct references to the sixth form in both **full** and **short** inspections;

- decide how to sample sixth-form students' work for analysis by relevant team inspectors;

- plan the preliminary visit to focus more on sixth-form issues and to brief the school on how the sixth form will be inspected;

- decide how to deploy the inspection team.

Deploying the team

Careful deployment of the team is crucial. Plan the inspection to suit the school, taking into account the experience and specialisms of the team.

- In a **full** inspection, use the additional time for sixth-form evaluation flexibly to ensure the most effective coverage of sixth-form lessons, taking into account the need for additional discussions with staff and students.

- In a **short** inspection, advise the team about the best time to be in the school to maximise the opportunities for observations of the courses they are inspecting and, in the case of those dealing with other aspects, the availability of key staff.

- Agree well before the inspection the days when team inspectors will be in school. You should be in the position to let the school know before the inspection begins which days inspectors will be on site.

- The lay inspector must play a full part in the inspection of the sixth form, particularly in bringing a lay perspective to important aspects such as the advice, support and guidance of students, and leadership and management.

Ensure that the evidence and judgements about the sixth form are treated as an entity but contribute to the findings about the school as a whole. You may find it helpful to have a member of the team to support you. This team member might accompany you on the preliminary visit. If you use someone to help you to co-ordinate the sixth-form evidence and findings, remember that **you have responsibility for the inspection as a whole,** and that your role is to ensure whole-school and sixth-form findings are fully integrated.

Work sample

The school will need guidance on how to select the students whose work will be analysed in each of the subjects or courses inspected in detail. The following pointers may help.

- Inspectors should see the work of a sample of students from each year group representing the range of attainment within the year.

- As far as possible, the work should be representative of different groups of students in the sixth form; follow up any issues you may have identified in your pre-inspection commentary.

- The work analysed should include notes, examples of assignments, completed answers, or other work that show how students work independently and apply their knowledge and skills.

- Look at the sample of work alongside students' records of assessment, where possible.

Some booklets in the series *Inspecting Subjects and Courses Post-16* give guidance on the kinds of work it is useful to see in particular subjects.

Inspections spanning two weeks

Short inspections will extend over a longer period than previously, and some short and full inspections may span two weeks. Some subject inspection may need to be outside the main part of the inspection. The main findings cannot be agreed until all first-hand evidence has been gathered, so ensure that any inspection outside the main part of the inspection takes place beforehand.

Inspecting a school that is part of a sixth-form consortium

In most circumstances you will be able to inspect in detail subjects and courses in the 'home' school, but where significant provision is made for students on other sites it must be inspected. With careful planning it should be possible for this to be done by a few inspectors.

Make sure that other schools where work will be inspected are aware of it, and that procedures are clear and agreed before the inspection. Points to remember are:

- evaluations of provision in other schools, and the standards achieved by students in the school being inspected form part of the overall evidence about the sixth form;

- feedback should be offered to teachers after lessons;

- subject feedback is offered to the school being inspected, but the headteacher can invite whom he or she wishes, subject to the registered inspector's agreement. This might include the head of subject in another school where a substantial amount of work has been seen.

The practical details of where and how to find lessons in other schools should be worked out before the inspection, so that inspectors' time is not wasted.

Team inspectors

You will notice few changes in a **full** inspection, but more in a **short** inspection.

In a **full** inspection, you must:

- include a sixth-form focus in the pre-inspection part of your Notebook, including an analysis and interpretation of available subject performance data;

- highlight sixth-form and main-school judgements and views separately, as you complete your Notebook during the inspection;

- complete the additional grades on the subject JRF for sixth-form subjects that are inspected and reported in detail.

In a **short** inspection, ensure that:

- you use a Notebook for any sixth-form subject inspected, including the JRF for any subjects inspected in detail;

- when taking responsibility for an aspect, use a Notebook for the sixth form, even if you decide not to use a Notebook for the short inspection of aspects in Key Stages 3 and 4.

Planning inspection time

In both **full and short** inspections, maximise the observation and discussion time you have for the sixth form by identifying the best days and times for subject inspection. Plan your sixth-form observations first. Agree these with the registered inspector well before the inspection.

Aim to spend the **equivalent** of one day inspecting an A-level subject or GNVQ course. This should be made up of:

- the observation of at least four lessons, where possible, for a sufficient length of time to form secure judgements, particularly of teaching and learning;

- analysis of students' work from both years in two-year courses;

- analysis of a sample of students' records;

- analysis of subject documentation, including any performance data not available before inspection such as any analyses of results of different groups of students;

- discussions with staff and students about post-16 work.

In some cases, particularly in **short** inspections, you may need to be in the school at a different time from most other team members to ensure coverage of your subject. Make sure that arrangements are in place for your evidence and judgements to contribute to the main part of the inspection, either through the registered inspector or by attendance at a team meeting.

☐ During the inspection

Registered inspector

Your main task will be to bring together whole-school and sixth-form judgements, giving appropriate weight to each.

In a **full** inspection:

- you should see little difference from full inspections up to September 2001, except that sixth-form issues will now be evaluated and discussed in more detail;

- ensure that the additional sixth-form JRF grades are completed.

In a **short** inspection:

- you will have a more substantial evidence base for the sixth form than for Key Stages 3 and 4;

- focus strongly on whole-school judgements, especially relating to Key Stages 3 and 4, while making a detailed evaluation of the sixth form. Take care to give appropriate weight to sixth-form judgements when you come to whole-school judgements;

- keep track of whole-school and sixth-form issues separately in the RCJ.

Your quality assurance role will be greater in an enhanced inspection. It will need careful management, particularly where team inspectors are in school for a short time.

In a **short** inspection, once you have come to your conclusions about each aspect of the *Schedule*, you only need to grade the whole-school features highlighted in bold typeface in the JRF. But complete the detailed judgement recording statements for the sixth form. Take care not to allow the sixth-form grades to unduly influence your whole-school grades.

Team meetings

In a **full** inspection:

- ensure that there is a clear emphasis on sixth-form evaluations, and that they contribute appropriately, but not disproportionately, to whole-school decisions.

In a **short** inspection:

- the management of team meetings is more of a challenge;

- keep a strong focus on the whole school, but make sure you allocate time for a detailed discussion on the sixth form;

- where team inspectors are not present at team meetings because their inspection is completed, make sure that their evidence and judgements are available so that they contribute to sixth-form and whole-school judgements;

- ensure that all the evidence related to aspects of the sixth form is effectively co-ordinated so that conclusions can be securely reached at the end of the inspection.

There is no single 'right way' to organise team meetings. Possibilities include:

- focusing some meetings on sixth-form issues;

- having 'two-part' meetings;

- adopting a more integrated approach to meetings.

In short inspections, it is crucial that the core team brings together the whole school judgements at the end of the inspection.

Team inspectors

Make sure:

- you have sufficient evidence to make secure and reliable judgements on the subjects you inspect in detail and to account for what is achieved by all students, and that you have sampled a range of work in the rest of the curriculum area;

- you secure evidence for the different levels and different year groups of the subject;

- you use *Inspecting Subjects and Courses Post-16* to help you make judgements about standards, achievement, teaching and learning in your subject.

In a **full** inspection, plan your sixth-form and Key Stages 3 and 4 observations to get the best possible coverage.

In a **short** inspection:

- if you are part of the core team, you will have the flexibility to see sixth-form work in your subject throughout the inspection, but you should still plan your observations carefully;

- if you join the inspection for only a short time, you are more restricted in what you can see. Get the best possible coverage you can. Where you are unable to see more than, say, three lessons, ensure you have sufficient evidence from other sources.

Feedback to teachers

Offer feedback after lessons in both **full** and **short** inspections.

In a **full** inspection, your subject feedback to the head of department should include specific references to the sixth form.

In a **short** inspection, you will only give feedback on those sixth-form subjects and courses you have inspected. If you are a 'core team' member you are likely to have seen some lessons in your subject in Key Stages 3 and 4. Resist any pressure from the school to give feedback on individual subjects pre-16, as that is not part of your remit. But ensure that teachers have feedback on their work so that the school benefits from your inspection.

In team meetings, reflect on the impact of the evidence from your subject on the whole-school issues being discussed.

☐ After the inspection

Registered and team inspectors

At the final team meeting, get the balance right between the sixth form and the main school especially in **short** inspections. This applies both to **registered inspectors** when managing the final team meeting, and to **team inspectors** in knowing what to contribute to the whole-school debate.

As a team, consider whether the school has an adequate sixth form; guidance on this is included in Part 5 of this *Supplement*. The judgement is linked to, but separate from, those about special measures, serious weaknesses and underachieving schools. All members of the team may not be at the final meeting. If you are the **registered inspector** ensure you have team members' findings and views before they leave the inspection.

Feedback to senior management and the governing body

If you are the **registered inspector,** consider the best way to structure your feedback to senior managers and governors to ensure that you present the findings for the school as a whole yet give sufficient weight to the sixth form.

In **full** inspections, despite the greater focus on the sixth form, reassure them that you are making judgements about the school as a whole.

In **short** inspections, structure your feedback so that the whole-school findings as well as the detailed feedback on the sixth form are clear. You may want to cover the sixth form separately and first, or to integrate your judgements throughout.

Part 4

Using the *Evaluation Schedule*

This part provides guidance on using the modified inspection *Schedule*. The guidance is similar in structure to that in the *Handbook for Inspecting Secondary Schools* in the following ways.

- The **evaluation schedule** sets out the judgements to be made and evaluation criteria to be used when you inspect the sixth form. The Schedule in *Inspecting Schools* should be used for Key Stages 3 and 4. Text in blue shows where there are differences between the two *Schedules*. For the most part, the same criteria are applied in the main school and the sixth form, but there are a few additional ones for the sixth form.

- The **inspection focus** amplifies the evaluation requirements stressing the features you should concentrate on in the sixth form.

- The section on **making judgements** deals with bringing evidence together. As in the *Handbook for Inspecting Secondary Schools*, the characteristics of very good, satisfactory and unsatisfactory provision and outcomes are to help you pitch your judgements.

- The **reporting requirements** set out how to include sixth-form features in the whole-school inspection report.

- **Further guidance** deals with interpreting and applying the criteria in the sixth-form context.

Note. Sections in Part 4 follow the numbering system used in the *Handbook for Inspecting Secondary Schools* and do not include sections 8 and 9.

1. What sort of school is it?

Inspectors must report on:

☐ the characteristics of the sixth form;

and evaluate and summarise:

☐ the effectiveness of the sixth form, including its cost-effectiveness;

☐ the main strengths and weaknesses of the sixth form;

☐ the extent to which the sixth form has improved, or not, since the last inspection;

relating their findings to the specific nature of the school.

Sixth-form inspection focus

The sixth-form Annex to the Summary of the Report is mainly for current and potential students. Make sure it gives them a clear and succinct picture of the sixth form, its effectiveness including cost-effectiveness, what standards and the quality of provision are like in different subjects, how well students are supported and guided, and their views of the sixth form.

Making judgements

☐ Characteristics of the sixth form

Set the scene of the sixth form to give a context for the inspection findings. In the summary this can be brief, but should be more detailed in its sixth-form annex. Comment on:

- the size of the sixth form;
- the nature of provision, including any collaborative arrangements with other schools;
- the background of students, their prior attainment, and how students of different gender, ethnic groups are represented;
- the proportions of students who 'stay on' from Year 11 and who transfer from other schools;
- any qualifications required for entry into the sixth form;
- the extent to which the sixth form is growing or otherwise;
- any recent changes in the nature of its provision.

☐ The effectiveness of the sixth form

The team must form a summative view about the effectiveness of the sixth form, and whether it is cost-effective. The judgement about effectiveness is based primarily on:

- what students achieve – drawing particularly on value-added indicators, the results in examinations and the standards seen in subjects and courses across the curriculum areas;
- the quality of teaching – in particular how it accounts for what is achieved;
- how far the sixth form is improving or maintaining high achievement – based on trends in performance in recent years.

Also take account of other factors that affect the quality of students' experience and success in the sixth form, such as how well they are advised, guided and supported and the quality of the curriculum and how well it meets their needs.

Features that detract from effectiveness include:

- undue variation in performance between subjects or between particular groups of students, with no convincing or well-founded explanations;
- a significant number of students not completing courses without good reason;
- sporadic or poor attendance such that achievement is not as high as it could be.

Cost-effectiveness

If students are achieving at least as well as expected, are taught well, and the sixth form is operating within its intended costs with no significant wastefulness or detrimental effects elsewhere in the school, it is **cost-effective**. Being cost-effective is not compatible with unsatisfactory performance.

Use similar principles to those you would use to evaluate 'value for money' for the school as a whole.

Inadequate sixth forms

If, as a team, you judge that the school has an 'inadequate sixth form' because its provision and effectiveness are not good enough, the judgement must be included in the summary report. Guidance on making and reporting the judgement is in Part 5 of this *Supplement*.

☐ **The main strengths and weaknesses**

The main strengths and areas for improvement of the sixth form **as a whole** agreed by the team will be summarised in the annex to the summary report. Their relative weight will reflect the overall effectiveness of the sixth form. The areas for improvement should be lead to issues for action relating to the sixth form in the report section '*What the school should do to improve*'.

Each subject section in Part E of the report includes the main strengths and areas for improvement in the subject or course. The most significant, or features that are common across a number of subjects, will contribute to the strengths and areas for improvement of the sixth form as a whole. The strengths and areas for improvement in subject areas should help subject improvement planning.

☐ **Improvement in the sixth form**

The previous report may include relatively little about the sixth form. Use the trail of information, including growth in the sixth form, examination results, any value-added data and developments in what the sixth form offers to make a brief comment about how well it is improving or continuing to perform very well.

Reporting requirements

Report section	Full and short inspections
1. What sort of school is it?	In both types of inspection, the context of the sixth form and the evaluations are included in the annex to the summary of the report.
	Brief comments about the sixth form should be included in the Summary of the report on the school **as a whole**. The sixth-form annex includes more detail, especially about standards and quality in subjects and courses.

An example of a sixth-form annex is included in Part 6.

2. How high are standards?

2.1 The school's results and achievements

Inspectors must interpret and report on:

☐ the school's results and other performance data post-16 (including retention rates and value-added data), highlighting any variations of achievement by different groups of students and in different subjects;

☐ trends in results over time;

☐ the school's progress towards its targets, including comment on whether the targets are sufficiently challenging.

Inspectors must evaluate and report on:

☐ standards of work seen, highlighting strengths and weaknesses in what students know, understand and can do;

- in all the subjects and courses inspected, focusing on students nearest the end of their courses, such as AS or A level;
- in the key skills of communication, application of number and IT, where relevant;
- highlighting variations between different groups of students and between subjects;

☐ how well students achieve, taking account of the progress they have made, their progress towards any individual goals or targets, the level of demand made of them and other relevant factors.

In determining their judgements, inspectors should consider, where relevant, the extent to which:

- the results in examinations and accreditations match or exceed the average for all schools;
- the school is either maintaining very high standards or improving as expected;
- the school sets challenging targets and is on course to meet or exceed them;
- students with special educational needs, having English as an additional language or who are gifted and talented, are making good progress;
- standards are consistently high across subjects;
- there are no significant differences in the standards achieved by students of different gender or ethnic background;
- results show significant added value in relation to students' earlier results;
- students' attainment meets or exceeds the levels set by any examination or assessment objectives;
- students reach appropriate levels in the key skills to meet individual students' needs;
- students successfully progress to relevant and appropriate higher education or employment.

Sixth-form inspection focus

Pursue the same three strands as in the main school:

- the interpretation of results, including trends over time;
- the evaluation of the standards of work seen; that is, how they compare with what is typically seen and expected irrespective of starting-points;
- the evaluation of achievement; that is, whether students are doing as well as they can taking account of what they have achieved before and their capability.

Use the guidance in the *Handbook for Inspecting Secondary Schools*, page 23, as your starting point.

Interpret the results for the sixth form as a whole **and** for different subjects and courses, identifying any variations among different groups of students.

Value-added analyses, comparing GCSE and post-16 accreditation results, provide powerful evidence in evaluating achievement. Take full account of them. Other indicators of success in the sixth form come from completion or retention data, and the destinations of students. Keep in mind how well students are prepared for the next stage of education, training or employment, and how successful they are in achieving their goals.

In your evaluation of standards and achievement, do not lose sight of students as individuals. Track a sample of students, seeing how well they are doing in relation to their background, aspirations and targets. Refer to the guidance in *Evaluating Educational Inclusion*, page 5.

Greater emphasis is now being given to key skills. Where they are being taught for the key skills qualification, evaluate the standards achieved, particularly in communication, application of number and information technology. Schools should not be criticised for not specifically teaching key skills towards the key skills qualifcation.

Making judgements

Before the inspection, use the Pre-inspection Context and School Indicator (PICSI) and Sixth-form Performance and Assessment (PANDA) reports and any other information about students' performance. Form an initial view about **standards** across the sixth form as a whole and in individual subjects, identifying any variations for different groups of students. Set your views alongside the school's evaluation in Form S4. Note any explanations the school offers for its results and any variations. Assess whether these explanations are well founded and convincing.

You may have information from the school's monitoring of performance before inspection, but, if not, make full use of it during the inspection. Schools increasingly carry out analyses that give insights, for example, into how successful different groups of students have been and value added from one stage to another. Use any value-added analyses as a starting-point for evaluating **achievement**.

If the school has not undertaken such analyses, do not ask for them to be done. Do what you can with whatever is available, and carry out sample analyses where possible. Annexes B and C include guidance on interpreting data and value-added analyses.

The school is likely to have information about the numbers of students embarking on and completing courses. Take note of patterns of recruitment and retention among different groups of students. Significant drop-out after a reasonable settling-in period must be set against what might appear to be a strong performance in the final examinations.

During inspection, use lesson observations, analysis of students' work, discussions with them and assessment records to establish the standards of current work and whether students are achieving as well as they can.

You must know and understand the specifications for courses to be able to evaluate the standards reached. When judging **standards**, match the work you see against the subject and course objectives and grade descriptions, as well as what you know of the expected standards in your subject.

Test students on what they know and understand, and assess the skills they show. Critical evaluation, research and analysis lie at the heart of post-16 advanced level work, and you need to evaluate whether these skills are being adequately developed.

Analyses of the GCSE results of students in the sixth form will indicate the baseline against which to set your observations during inspection. Be cautious about their use until you are able to verify that the profile is representative of students taking sixth-form courses and the pattern of take-up of subjects. Identify a sample of students following specific courses and compare what they are currently achieving with what they achieved at 16+.

Value-added measures and current standards set against students' GCSE background, that is, the progress students make, contribute to the evaluation of **achievement.** But form a professional view by assessing whether students are being sufficiently stretched. Assess whether the targets being set and the demands on students are such that they are all working at full stretch.

Report any differences between the achievements of different groups of students in relation to gender, ethnicity or special needs. Assess whether the reasons given by the school are well founded and convincing.

Ensure that you reconcile and explain differences between standards as indicated by performance data and what you observe.

The following characteristics illustrate where to pitch your judgements about standards and students' achievement in the sixth form.

	Standards	Achievement
High or above (standards) **Very good or better** (achievement)	Average points scores for each student and average points score in subject entries are well above the national averages. Knowledge and skills are very well developed, well beyond what might typically be expected.	Most students are working at full stretch and achieving very well. Value-added studies show that most students make more progress than their baseline performance would suggest, and no groups underachieve. Retention rates and success rates in reaching targets and goals are high.
Average or above (standards) **Satisfactory or better** (achievement)	Average points scores are at least in line with the national averages. Most students demonstrate the knowledge, understanding and skills at least in line with what the average student might be expected to achieve.	Most students are working well and are achieving as expected. Value-added studies indicate that most students are making progress in line with their baseline prospects. Most students are successful in achieving their higher education or employment goals. Retention is good.

Features likely to indicate unsatisfactory achievement include:

- underachievement by particular groups of students, notably the most able, male versus female students, those with special educational needs or minority ethnic students, for which there is no well-founded or convincing explanation;
- students' achievements in the key skills are too low for them to cope adequately with their studies or for them to have reasonable prospects of meeting the demands of further education and/or employment.

Reporting requirements

Report on standards and achievement in the sixth form as follows:

Report section	Full inspections	Short inspections
2.1 The school's results and students' achievements.	Use a **subheading 'sixth form'** within this section of the report.	Include a section on **'The school's results and students' achievements'** in Part D of the report

When reporting on standards and achievement, begin with a brief interpretation of the results and other data, and follow this with your evaluation of standards seen in current students' work and how well students are achieving. Highlight any strengths and weakness in results or in what you see. Ensure that any differences between standards as seen in results and in current work are explained.

Guidance on using criteria

Use the booklets in the series *Inspecting Subjects and Courses Post-16* to evaluate standards and achievement in individual subjects.

☐ Sixth-form results and other performance data

Do the school's results in examinations and accreditations match or exceed the average for all schools? Are standards consistently high across subjects?

Comparison of performance with national averages, whether overall or for specific subjects, is difficult because of the variability in the make-up of sixth forms and groups within them. Nonetheless, use average points scores, and percentages of students gaining grades A–B and grades A–E as the main yardsticks for forming a view about the standards achieved by the school and in subjects. Where sixth-form numbers are small use rolling averages over several years as well as the results of individual years, and note trends over time.

PICSI and PANDA reports currently include the average points scores for students taking two or more A-level courses or equivalent, and less than two. An interpretation of the average points score for students taking two or more A-level courses is included in the summary report. National comparison data are provided, but because of the individuality of sixth forms, there are no comparisons with similar schools. The composition of sixth forms can vary because of many factors, not least the requirements for entry to the sixth form.

While evaluating standards is important, the crucial question is whether the standards are as high as they should be given the prior attainment of pupils. Value-added measures give a starting-point in answering this question. Increasingly more data will be available, particularly about individual subjects. Use value-added data fully in forming a picture of how students are performing.

In sixth forms that operate collaboratively with other institutions, some results will be the consequence of teaching elsewhere. Take this into account when commenting on the results particularly where there is a marked disparity between subjects or courses. Consider the school's examination results alongside those of the consortium as a whole. The inspection is intended to focus on how well students in the school being inspected are doing and the provision made for them in the 'home' school or elsewhere. If there is high mobility, such that there is a significant influx of new students into the sixth form, ask the school for evidence of these students' attainment when they enter the school and judge what effect, if any, this has on overall performance.

To make sensible comparisons across subjects, establish the composition of groups taking different subjects, noting any significant variations.

Guidance on interpreting examination results for the school as a whole and in individual subjects is in annex B.

Continuation and completion of courses

Students' success in seeing courses through to completion, in meeting demanding targets and goals, and success in moving on to higher education or employment as is appropriate for them, provide indicators of achievement. Schools will often have data about the proportions of students who continue with their courses to final accreditation. The 'baseline' numbers of those starting courses are usually those after the first half-term, to allow for the inevitable changes of mind.

Where students do not continue, explore the reasons. Determine whether they are sensible and valid, and how students responded to any guidance provided by the school. It is necessary to distinguish between students:

- who leave early because decisions made at the entry to the sixth form were wrong;
- who have simply lost interest or have not been able to cope with the work;
- for whom an alternative and possibly better opportunity has presented itself.

Guard against presenting findings about retention and continuity in a way that suggests that changes of plan leading to students leaving the sixth form early is a mark of failure on the part of the school, unless the proportion affected is high or it disproportionately affects particular groups of students. Also, a high level of completion alone may not be a measure of success; some students may be on a course too low for them. Nonetheless, retention rates provide a basis for questions that the inspection should pursue.

There are, as yet, no national benchmarks for retention on courses in schools. Typically, retention is very high. Explore any significant variations between subjects and groups of students. Test whether the school's explanations are well founded and convincing. Explore how well recruitment and retention are monitored for the school to be able to take appropriate action.

Retention rates can reflect not only on the quality of teaching, but the quality of support and guidance, including advice before students embark on their sixth-form programmes, the curriculum provision, the attitudes of students to their work and local employment circumstances.

Value added

Do results show significant added value in relation to students' earlier results?

Value-added measures, comparing, for example, A-level and GCSE results for the same students, give a strong starting-point for hypotheses about achievement.

The school may have detailed value-added information. If not, compare the average or total points scores for GCSE, if they are known, and the advanced level scores (including any AS or advanced vocational courses, if applicable) of a sample of students representing different levels of prior attainment. Take care when comparing the GCSE points score of the school with that of the sixth form; extensive mobility makes comparisons difficult because the GCSE score includes pupils who have left at 16+ and will not include those students who have joined the sixth form from other schools.

Most schools that take monitoring of their performance seriously will have some analyses of their results. Fully use whatever is available.

In assessing the value added by the sixth form and in individual subjects, take account of the entry qualifications not only for the sixth form as a whole, but also differences from subject to subject including any minimum entry requirements. The key requirement is to evaluate the effectiveness of provision in subjects given the prior attainment of students embarking on the courses. Look at the pattern of take-up for different subjects. Guidance on calculating and interpreting value-added measures is in annex C.

☐ Trends in results over time

Is the school maintaining very high standards or improving as expected?

The interpretation of overall and subject results over time can be problematic. Apparent trends in performance need to be checked carefully to ensure comparability in the make-up of the groups of students that obtained the results.

Where small numbers are involved, the performance of two or three students will have a substantial impact on the overall result for the group. Quite small changes in group composition may well produce large shifts between years; carefully consider judgements about trends in this light. Take a view over as long a period as you can and use rolling averages where you can.

☐ Standards of work seen

Does students' attainment meet or exceed the levels set by examination or assessment objectives? Are there significant differences in the standards achieved by students of different gender or ethnic background?

Evaluate standards in relation to what is expected for the course and its level. Take account of how long students have spent on it. Identify and explain any significant differences in standards for different groups of students taking the same or similar courses.

Subject specifications include objectives, prescribed content and grade descriptions. Use them, as well as your professional knowledge, to assess standards. The 'average grade' achieved in most subjects at A-level is C–D; use this as a benchmark, but refer to the average points score for individual subjects.

Highlight any strengths or weaknesses in what students know, understand and can do. In particular, include the evaluation of skills that become increasingly dominant in advanced-level work, such as research, critical analysis and problem-solving.

Key skills

Do students reach appropriate levels in the key skills?

Where key-skills teaching is being directed specifically towards accreditation, focus on the standards achieved, particularly in the main skills.

The extent to which schools enter students for the key-skills qualifications will vary. As results become available, use them as part of your evaluation of the standards reached. Some schools will have 'in-house' schemes for promoting and assessing key skills.

Subject specifications identify opportunities for key-skill development and the level of skills expected. In advanced-level courses, key skills are specified at level 3. Whether or not key skills are specifically taught, assess how well students are able to cope with the key-skill demands of their subject courses. Assess, for example, students' capacity to make and take notes, to digest the material they read, to present their findings coherently, to handle mathematics including statistics, and to make effective use of information and communication technology. You must report where students' skills are insufficient to cope with the courses they are following; equally, where they are particularly strong, highlight how they enhance work in the subject.

The wider key skills of working with others, study skills, and problem-solving are important components of students' learning and attitudes to school and you should evaluate these aspects of their work.

☐ How well do students achieve?

Are students successful in progressing to relevant and appropriate higher education or employment? Do students with special educational needs, having English as an additional language or who are gifted and talented, make good progress?

Value-added indicators give a starting-point in evaluating how well students are doing. These usually relate to students that have left the school. The work of current students set against their previous record of attainment gives a more up-to-date view.

In discussions with students, assess what they are capable of by challenging them to show how far they can extend their thinking beyond their immediate work, and evaluate how well their potential matches what teachers expect of them. When you sample students' work, focus on material that shows the level of students' thinking and capacity for determined and persistent problem-solving. Assess whether the work you see demonstrates the progress and level of challenge that you would expect and reflects individual students' learning needs.

Some groups of students may be achieving less well than others. Make sure you follow up any issues raised by analysing and interpreting data fully and by observation. Test any explanations offered by the school.

2.2 Students' attitudes, values and personal development

Inspectors must evaluate and report on students':

☐ attitudes to the school;

☐ behaviour, including the incidence of exclusions;

☐ personal development and relationships;

☐ attendance.

In determining their judgements, inspectors should consider the extent to which students:

- are keen and eager to come to school;
- show interest in school life, and are involved in the range of activities the school provides;
- behave well in lessons and around the school and are courteous, trustworthy and show respect for property;
- form constructive relationships with one another, and with teachers and other adults;
- work in an atmosphere free from oppressive behaviour, such as bullying, sexism and racism;
- reflect on what they do, and understand its impact on others;
- respect other people's differences, particularly their feelings, values and beliefs;
- show initiative and are willing to take responsibility;
- develop the attitudes and skills necessary to maintain lifelong learning, including the capacity to work independently, to study and to work with others;
- have high levels of attendance.

Sixth Form Inspection Focus

Focus on the personal development of students and how well, over their time in the sixth form, students develop the attitudes and skills to enable them to meet the demands of the next stage of their lives. This includes:

- taking increasing responsibility for themselves, for example through the development of key skills, such as working with other people and independent study;
- the development of positive attitudes to learning that are likely to sustain their interest in continuing education and training well into working life.

Spiritual, moral, social and cultural development continue to be important. Evaluate the contribution that life in the sixth form, enrichment activities and the subjects studied make to these aspects of personal development, and students' attitudes to them.

Consider the relationship between the sixth form and the rest of the school. In particular, observe the extent to which students and pupils contribute to and benefit from the life of the school as a whole as well as from the sixth form.

While post-16 education is not compulsory, regular and punctual attendance contributes greatly to learning. Identify and evaluate any poor or irregular attendance and poor punctuality, and ways in which they affect the quality of work.

Making judgements

Observe students in different contexts, such as lessons, self-study, extra-curricular activities, and in events that students have been responsible for. Talk to as many as possible. Use the evidence from any surveys carried out by the school, including the student's questionnaire.

The following characteristics illustrate where to pitch judgements about the attitudes, values and personal development of students.

Very good or better	Students are avid workers and make the most of the opportunities available. They are keen to take responsibility for and participate in activities. Relationships with one another and staff are positive and constructive, and students show a high level of respect for the feelings, values and beliefs of others. Their thirst to do well is evident in lessons, study time, in following up assessments of their work. They contribute positively to the ethos of the school and are a good and helpful influence on younger pupils. Students can argue a case and show respect for evidence. They have strong perceptions of their role as members of the school and as citizens. Attendance is very high. The vast majority of students have well developed attitudes and skills to enable them to continue learning in adult life, with a capacity to work independently.
Satisfactory or better	Students do the work that is asked of them, and many go beyond. They are co-operative, willing to help each other and members of staff, and many take part in activities outside lessons. Relationships are harmonious. There is little absence and most students complete the courses they have embarked on. Most show independence in their study.

Features likely to indicate that students' attitudes and personal development are unsatisfactory include:

- careless or casual attitudes evidenced by a significant amount of uncompleted work;
- work done at a minimal level which only just satisfies the teacher's requirement;
- high levels of absenteeism or sloppy punctuality;
- excessive dependence on teachers, doing only what the teacher asks;
- failure on the part of students to take responsibility for their work or show any initiative;
- evidence of bullying, racist attitudes or lack of respect for others;
- lack of participation in the school as a community;
- reluctance to see how their school work will contribute to their adult life.

Reporting Requirements

Report on students' attitudes, values and personal development in the sixth form as follows:

Report section	Full inspections	Short inspections
2.2 Students' attitudes, values and personal development.	Use the subheading 'sixth form' within this section.	Include a section on 'Students' attitudes, values and personal development' in Part D of the report.

Guidance on using the criteria

☐ Students' attitudes to school

Do students show interest in school life, and their work, and are they involved in the range of activities the school provides?

If the school has chosen to use the student's questionnaire it will give you an initial view of how students feel about the sixth form, and issues to follow up. The school may also have provided evidence from its own surveys. Discussions and observations in lessons, study sessions, enrichment activities and around the school generally and analysis of students' work provide evidence for judgements.

Compare and evaluate the relationship between:

- students' attitudes to their work and their enthusiasm for and involvement in it;
- their involvement in the life of the school as a whole and the range of activities outside study that the school, and students themselves, organise.

Some schools have a vibrant range of activities to enrich the curriculum and provide opportunities for social activity, community service, outdoor pursuits, leadership development, complementary study, spiritual and cultural development, and so on. See how far students embrace these opportunities as well as pursuing their studies.

Students' response to assemblies, their tutors and the support they are given, together with unprogrammed study time and how productively they use it are indicators of their approach to sixth-form work.

☐ Personal development and relationships

Do students develop the attitudes and skills necessary to maintain lifelong learning, including the capacity to work independently, to study and to work with others?

Aspects of personal development identified in the *Handbook for the Inspection of Secondary Schools,* pages 41 and 42, continue to be important in the sixth form, in particular those associated with spiritual, moral, social and cultural development.

In the sixth form, pay attention also to how far students have developed the attitudes and skills that will fit them for higher education and employment. Evaluate, for example, the extent to which students:

- work together effectively in groups of different size and composition, showing respect for each other's viewpoints;

- are supportive of each other, and look for ways to help those who may be experiencing difficulties;

- are willing to take responsibility, whether this is for themselves or in planning and organising activities with others;

- are able and prepared to take initiative and behave as 'self-starters', rather than waiting for others to tell them what they should do;

- can work independently and pursue problems without easily 'giving in', yet at the same time know when collaborative effort or seeking help would be beneficial;

- reflect on and discuss their own feelings, beliefs and experiences;

- are receptive to new ideas and fresh viewpoints and willing to consider views and beliefs other than their own;

- develop positive long-term attitudes to their continuing education;

- understand issues related to equal opportunities and promoting good personal, community and race relations.

Some of these characteristics make up the wider key skills of working with others, study skills and problem-solving. They impinge on learning skills that will also be part of your evaluation of teaching and learning.

☐ **Attendance**

Do students have high levels of attendance?

Benchmarks for attendance are not available for sixth-form students, but attendance should certainly be no lower than that for Key Stage 4. Regular attendance is crucial in lessons and timetabled self-study sessions. Courses post-16, particularly one-year courses to AS, have to cover substantial ground in a relatively short time. If there are more than isolated cases of unexplained or irregular attendance, or if attendance in any way seems to be a contributory factor to lower achievement, investigate and report. Pay particular attention to any undue variations between different groups of students. Make links to the quality of support and guidance and how effectively the school is dealing with any problems. Be alert to how punctual students are, and how ready they are to work.

3. How well are students taught?

Inspectors must evaluate and report on:

☐ the quality of teaching, judged in terms of its impact on students' learning and what makes it successful or not.

Inspectors must include evaluations of:

- the teaching in the courses and subjects inspected, commenting on any variations between them;

- where relevant, how well the key skills of communication, application of number and IT are taught;

- how well the school meets the needs of all its students, taking account of age, gender, ethnicity, capability, special educational needs, gifted and talented students, and those for whom English is an additional language;

☐ how well students learn and make progress.

In determining their judgements, inspectors should consider the extent to which teachers:

- show good subject knowledge and understanding in the way they present and discuss their subject;

- plan effectively, setting clear objectives that students understand;

- challenge and inspire students expecting the most of them, so as to deepen their knowledge and understanding;

- use methods and styles of teaching which enable all students to learn effectively;

- manage students and their learning well, recognising their individual needs;

- use time, support staff and other resources, especially information and communication technology, effectively;

- ensure access to learning resources that are appropriate for effective independent study;

- assess students' work thoroughly and use assessments to help and encourage students to overcome difficulties;

- use homework and longer-term assignments effectively to reinforce and/or extend what is learned in school;

and the extent to which students:

- acquire new knowledge or skills, develop ideas and increase their understanding;

- apply intellectual, physical or creative effort in their work;

- are productive and work at a good pace;

- show interest in their work, are able to sustain concentration and think and learn for themselves;

- understand what they are doing, how well they have done and how they can improve.

Sixth-form inspection focus

The quality of teaching is the main determinant of how well students learn, their attitude to the subjects and courses they are studying, and what they achieve. Look out for teaching that has the quality to inspire and challenge at the highest level, and which demonstrates expertise or scholarship.

Teaching is judged by its effect on the quality of students' learning and their gains in knowledge, skills and understanding. Identify and report on teaching that works well and that which does not. In particular, assess whether it is good enough to give students a chance of achieving at the highest levels in advanced and other courses post-16.

Some sixth-form learning activities, such as self-study, research assignments and work placements, are not classroom based and do not involve direct teaching. These help to develop specific competencies needed for post-16 work. Ensure that non-classroom learning is evaluated.

Making judgements

Judgements are made about teaching and learning:

- in individual subjects and courses;
- across the sixth form as a whole.

Observe and evaluate teachers and students at work, discuss their work with them, analyse students' work and teachers' planning. Evaluate the impact of teaching on students' learning and how well they achieve; do not just check off individual criteria.

Teachers should recognise individual students' needs. Students have chosen to stay on after compulsory schooling to follow subjects and courses of their choice. Evaluate how effectively teaching meets the needs of all students, including those who are gifted or talented, those with special educational needs and those for whom English is an additional language. Evaluate whether teaching promotes equal opportunities and racial harmony.

Not all subjects and courses will be inspected in detail. You should, though, sample across all sixth-form work to contribute to the overall view of teaching and learning in the sixth form and to give a fair view of its strengths and weaknesses.

Judgements about teaching and learning are made using more than just evidence from lessons. A range of evidence is essential, especially in subjects where a relatively small number of lessons might be seen. Averaging of lesson grades, particularly in these circumstances, is not the way to arrive at judgements; for the sixth form as a whole, the profiles of teaching and learning grades have greater significance.

Good teaching is normally associated with good achievement, and good achievement with good teaching. Where this is not the case, you need to explain any incongruity.

Use booklets in the series *Inspecting Subjects and Courses Post-16* to guide your evaluation of teaching and learning in individual subjects and courses. These include examples of teaching that is very good, satisfactory and unsatisfactory to use as benchmarks.

The characteristics of very good or better, satisfactory or better and unsatisfactory teaching and learning in sixth forms have much in common with those that apply to the main school. However, the following are particularly important in the sixth form.

Very good or better	Work is very thoroughly prepared, but this does not prevent effective use of unanticipated opportunities that arise in the lessons. Teachers' enthusiasm for teaching the subject inspires students, and their authority and expertise challenge students. Over a period of time, the range of methods used is varied and stimulates a spectrum of learning skills, including students' capacity to make accurate and productive critical evaluations of their work. Assessment ensures that individual students know how well they are doing and how to improve. Students' work shows evidence of high-quality independent research, extended study and thinking. Teaching is effective in promoting these qualities, as well as in promoting highly responsive and productive working relationships.
Satisfactory or better	Subject content is accurate and is planned and presented clearly and effectively. Working methods are suitable for the task and enable students to make sufficient progress. Lessons have clear objectives and students know what they are doing, with a sufficient overview of the structure of the work to be able to plan their use of time sensibly. Their work is marked regularly and thoroughly, and comments help them to understand where they have gone wrong and what to do about it. They respond positively and purposefully in lessons, answering questions readily. There may be signs of over-dependence on teachers, but they know this and take steps to challenge students' thinking and develop their capacity for independent study and research.

Features likely to indicate that teaching is unsatisfactory include:

- the teacher's command of the subject is insufficient and does not promote challenging work at the level demanded by the course;

- assessment and review are inadequate and do not give students a clear and critical picture of their achievement and progress in the subject. They do not have an adequate understanding of what to do to make improvements;

- the teaching methods do not allow students to attain the course objectives; for example, over-didactic teaching makes too little demand on students' initiative and research;

- failure to provide adequately for individual learning needs.

Reporting requirements

Report on teaching and learning in the sixth form as follows:

Report section	Full inspections	Short inspections
3. How well are students taught?	Use a subheading **'sixth form'** and use this subsection to report your findings on the sixth form. This does not preclude a brief comment in the introductory part of the section.	Include a section on **'How well are students taught?'** in Part D of the report.

Guidance on using the criteria

☐ **How well students learn**

Do students acquire new knowledge or skills, develop ideas and increase their understanding? Do they apply intellectual, physical or creative effort in their work?

Sixth-form work should markedly advance students' knowledge, understanding and skills beyond those acquired in Key Stage 4, particularly where they are following level 3 courses. Ensure that students are covering enough new ground and pushing their knowledge and understanding on enough in the early stages of AS courses. Where students have the potential, they might be challenged to tackle AEA papers.

Students should show increasing capacity for research, critical analysis, and the rigorous pursuit of ideas, assignments and problems to their conclusions. Over-dependence on teachers and work that is repetitive or superficial indicate that students are not learning as well as they can.

As you observe classes and talk with students, focus on individuals and judge whether they are working to their potential. Set this in the context of whether the school is catering effectively for its range of students, identifying their individual aspirations, aptitudes and needs, recruiting them onto the right courses and helping them to achieve as well as they can.

AS courses include a broader mix of students than would have been the case in the first year of A-level courses prior to September 2000. Not all students will aspire to A-level courses. Ensure that all are being suitably challenged and are gaining sufficient by teaching that recognises the differences in their prior attainment and potential.

Are students productive and do they work at a good pace? Do they show interest in their work, are they able to sustain concentration and think and learn for themselves?

These questions apply to students' work in and out of the classroom. Although study time is likely to be less in many schools than it was before the introduction of the broader curriculum in Year 12, students will spend some of their time in school away from the teacher. Evaluate how productively students use this time, whether they take full advantage of the resources available to them, for example, the library or information and communication technology, and how vigorously they pursue assignments. In discussion with students, evaluate how well they sustain their interest and determination to see problems through. There will be evidence in students' work of how quickly they give in and seek help.

☐ The quality of teaching, judged in terms of its impact on students' learning and what makes it successful or not

Do teachers show good subject knowledge and understanding in the way they present and discuss their subject? Do teachers challenge and inspire students, expecting the most of them, so as to deepen their knowledge and understanding?

Changes in the curriculum and subject and course specifications require teachers (and inspectors) to be up to date with current requirements.

Teachers' mastery of their subject at and beyond the level required for the courses they teach, and their up-to-date expertise in vocational areas ensure that students encounter and learn from scholarship and excellence. Deficiencies in subject knowledge and competence are likely to have a significant impact on what students achieve.

Teachers' knowledge and understanding of the subjects and courses they teach will be evident in:

- their exposition, and how they illuminate and explain ideas;

- the questions they ask and answer;

- their capacity to extend students' thinking beyond the routine or superficial and to push towards higher grades;

- their ability to draw on relevant vocational and other contexts, including diversity of culture, to develop students' understanding of concepts and their significance;

- their ability to present the subject effectively to students with different learning needs.

Good teaching sets high expectations and challenges students to believe in their ability to do well particularly at the beginning of, but also throughout, courses.

Faced with different styles of work in the sixth form, many students can experience a period of doubt and lack of confidence in being able to meet the new demands. Teaching should be sensitive to this, but at the same time help students to set themselves demanding and attainable targets. Give credit to teaching that is supportive and yet demanding.

Teachers' enthusiasm for their subject helps to shape students' approach to their studies and the effectiveness of their learning. This is particularly so in the sixth form, where students increasingly develop personal views and interpretations as well as extend their knowledge and skills.

Do teachers use methods and styles of teaching that enable all students to learn effectively? Do they ensure that students have access to learning resources appropriate for effective independent learning? Do they manage students and their learning well? Do teachers use homework, and longer-term assignments, effectively to reinforce and extend what is learned in school?

Sixth-form teaching should provide a bridge between the more structured context of school work pre-16 and the wider demands and expectations of independent work in higher education and employment.

More extended assignments and greater opportunities for research than in Key Stage 4 are essential for the development of skills in post-16 courses. Evaluate whether assignments are sufficiently well designed to extend and consolidate specific skills, knowledge and understanding, and to challenge students. Teachers should take account of the resources that are available for students so that assignments are manageable.

Judge how well teachers of vocational and other courses, such as business education or design and technology use simulated or real work-settings and effectively take learning out of the classroom.

Students may need to cover parts of their course through independent study. Your evaluation of teaching will include how well self-study materials are designed, access to resources and how well students are guided in their use. Whatever the balance between self-study and taught sessions, evaluate how regularly and how well learning is assessed and the steps teachers take to help students overcome problems.

Over a reasonable period of time, the range of methods used should be varied enough to help students acquire a range of learning skills and the knowledge, understanding and skills in their subjects or courses. Exposition and discussion will be a regular feature of lessons through which students gain knowledge and develop their understanding. Note how far both teachers and students ask probing questions, the extent to which they are given time to think about the questions before being expected to respond, and the quality of teachers' follow up to questions. Do they use sufficient open-ended questions to deny students the easy way out?

Lessons in the sixth form are often characterised by a more informal adult working relationship than occurs with younger pupils. Look closely at the consequences of this to ensure that it does not result in a lack of pace and demand in the teaching.

Teaching of key skills

Where key-skills teaching leads to accreditation, assess what you see in relation the school's policy; teachers should be clear about what is expected. Teaching should be to the national key-skills specifications/units which are currently available. Remember that the teaching of the key skills is optional; so the absence of teaching to a particular specification must not be criticised. Evaluate, though, whether students have the necessary skills to cope with their courses and the opportunities they have to develop their learning skills so they are prepared for learning beyond school.

4. How good are the curricular and other opportunities offered to students?

Inspectors must evaluate and report on:

☐ the quality and range of opportunities for learning provided for students and the extent to which these meet their individual needs, interests and aspirations;

including comment on:

- provision made for students to develop key skills, where the school has chosen to teach them;
- how responsive the school's provision is to local circumstances;
- enrichment studies and activities that provide for students' continued spiritual, moral, social and cultural development;
- work-related education, including careers education;
- the quality of links with the community and other schools and colleges, particularly where there is shared provision of sixth-form courses;

☐ whether the school meets statutory curricular requirements for religious education and collective worship.

In determining their judgements, inspectors should consider the extent to which the school:

- provides worthwhile opportunities which meet the interests, aptitudes and particular needs of students, including those having special educational needs;
- plans the curriculum and programmes of work that are coherent and allow students to progress well;
- provides enrichment through its curricular and extra-curricular provision, including support for learning outside the school day;
- is socially inclusive by ensuring equality of access and opportunity for all students;
- provides students with knowledge and insights into values and beliefs, and enables them to reflect on their experiences in a way which develops their spiritual awareness and self-knowledge;
- promotes principles which distinguish right from wrong;
- encourages students to take responsibility, show initiative and develop an understanding of living in a community;
- teaches students to appreciate their own cultural traditions and the diversity and richness of other cultures;
- provides effectively for personal and social education, including health education, sex education and attention to drug misuse;
- provides effective careers education, work experience, and vocational education;
- has links with the community which contribute to students' learning;
- effectively integrates any multi-site provision to give coherent programmes of learning;
- provide opportunities for students to develop key skills.

Sixth-form inspection focus

In the sixth form, the essential test of the quality and effectiveness of the curriculum is how well programmes and courses reflect the needs and interests of individual learners and enable them to achieve appropriate qualifications and skills for higher education or employment. In this, the school should be responsive to local circumstances.

Except in the largest sixth forms, schools are unlikely to be able to provide courses to meet the needs of all potential students. What is crucial is the help schools give students to find the courses they want in the institutions that provide them. Some schools have specialisms and meet particular local needs. Take these factors into account when evaluating the range of provision and how well it meets students' needs and aspirations.

Curriculum 2000 promotes greater breadth of study in Year 12, and the school's curriculum should allow this. This requires creativity and flexibility in timetabling.[7]

Provision to help students develop the key skills will vary. In many schools, provision will lead to accreditation. Whether or not this is the case, schools should be helping students to develop the skills they need to cope with their courses.

Enrichment programmes that enable students to broaden their horizons and extend their personal development feature in many sixth forms. Evaluate this dimension of the curriculum through sampling the programme and evaluating contributions that come through the teaching in subjects and courses.

The statutory requirements relating to collective worship and the teaching of religious education are as for the main school.

Making judgements

Pre-inspection evidence from the school's prospectus and visits to the school will set the scene of what the school intends to provide on its own or in collaboration with other schools or colleges. Assess the effect of the curriculum on students, including particular groups, on the choices they can make, the sixth-form experience as a whole, and how well subject or course planning and organisation contributes to their learning.

Find out how well the curriculum meets individual students' needs and aspirations by focusing on a cross-section of students. Examine their timetables and discuss them with the students. Assess their total workload and the extent to which their programme provides a considered balance between taught and private study time. Are they taking too many courses? Include what resources the school provides, outside the taught programme, for independent study through, for example, the use of ICT. Establish whether the curriculum is inclusive, promotes racial equality, and equality of opportunity and access to courses.

Evaluate how well course specifications are translated into coherent and well-designed programmes of work.

---

[7] See *Curriculum 2000: Implementing the Changes to 16–19 Qualifications* (Qualifications and Curriculum Authority 1999, Circular 42/99).

The following characteristics illustrate where to pitch judgements about the quality of opportunities for learning. Bear in mind and give due credit to the planning of the provision with other schools where sixth-form provision is shared.

Very good or better	The curriculum provides very well for students' needs and effectively complements other local provision. The school ensures that its students have the best possible advice about where they can access courses that the school cannot offer. The curriculum is tailored effectively to be consistent with the school's aims and the rationale for its sixth form. Planning is coherent and systematic, including the provision for developing key skills, where relevant. The curriculum is enhanced by enrichment activities that strongly contribute to students' personal development and opportunities to reflect on spiritual, moral, social and cultural issues relevant to them. Students' programmes are carefully monitored for coherence, and course planning ensures that students build on existing knowledge and experience. Careful thought is given to the provision of useful study time. Joint provision between schools is carefully planned, and its effectiveness is monitored.
Satisfactory or better	The school offers subjects and courses appropriate to students' needs, and ensures that students are aware of what is available in other schools and colleges in the area. The enrichment programme offers a satisfactory range of activities including sport. Where the school has chosen to teach the key skills, there is reasonable provision within subjects and the enrichment programme. The curriculum is inclusive and ensures equality of access and opportunity.

Features likely to indicate that the curriculum is unsatisfactory include:

- the curriculum is not well matched to the needs, capabilities and aspirations of the students;

- students' programmes of work are not effectively planned, managed and monitored, with the result that a significant number fail to make enough progress, drop out, or particular groups are disproportionately disadvantaged;

- students have few if any opportunities to broaden their experience beyond their subject work;

- little account is taken of the knowledge, skills and understanding needed for work outside school or for further training or higher education;

- where a consortium arrangement operates, planning that leads to fragmented programmes, wasted time and questionable benefit to students;

- the arrangements for non-taught time are ineffective, such that its use is unproductive;

- course planning in more than a few cases does not allow students to learn and make progress in a coherent way;

- the curriculum shows a lack of educational inclusiveness and denies equality of opportunity and access.

Reporting requirements

Report on the opportunities for learning that the school provides for its students as follows:

Report section	Full inspections	Short inspections
4. How good are the curricular and other opportunities offered to students?	Use a subheading '**sixth form**' within this section.	Include a section '**How good are the curricular and other opportunities offered to students?**' in Part D of the report.

Guidance on using the criteria

☐ **Range and quality of the curriculum**

Does the school provide worthwhile opportunities which meet the interests, aptitudes and particular needs of students? Is the curriculum inclusive by ensuring equality of access and opportunity for all students?

The range of subjects and courses available to students should give them scope to build on what they have already achieved and experienced in the 11–16 curriculum, as well as providing a range of choices and opportunities in new areas.

It is not necessary for an individual school to provide a vast range of courses. This may run counter to sensible economics and jeopardise provision elsewhere in the school or maintenance of quality in sixth form. The crucial requirements are that the rationale for the provision in the sixth form is clear, that course provision is consistent with its aims and that the quality of provision is good. A school may deliberately offer a narrow, specialist range of courses, but with clear knowledge of other complementary provision locally and openness in its co-operation with other schools or colleges. There must be secure guidance for students to ensure they can have ready access to the courses they need.

A small number of schools use the International Baccalaureate courses and qualifications in place of, or alongside, GCE. In evaluating a curriculum that includes these, use the same criteria of range, breadth and adequacy of combinations of subjects.

The destinations of leavers and the success of students on different types of examination courses provide pointers to the appropriateness of the sixth-form curriculum and to the effectiveness of guidance in Year 11.

Sixth-form size and its impact on the curriculum

In small sixth forms, the choice of courses is likely to be narrow, but the curriculum might still be carefully planned in relation to other provision locally or within a consortium. The range of provision is only one factor in the complex issue of providing a quality curriculum in a small sixth form which requires responsible management of resources across the school as a whole. You should have no pre-conceived view that a small sixth form is unsatisfactory. Judge each school's arrangements on its merits. The curriculum may be limited in scope but your prime concern is to assess its quality.

Some questions that are likely to arise in small sixth forms are:

- What is the impact on the quality of the curriculum as a whole and how well does it meet students' needs when courses that are offered do not run because of lack of numbers?

- How effective are strategies to cope with small numbers, such as joint Year 12–13 teaching?

- What is the quality of learning when students are working in very small groups?

The effectiveness of resource management in providing for small sixth forms should be considered as part of the evaluation of leadership and management.

Planning of courses and programmes

Does the school plan the curriculum and programmes of work that are coherent and allow students to progress? Does the school effectively integrate any multi-site provision to give a coherent programme of learning?

Schools will take different approaches to planning AS and A-level courses. Year 12 groups include students who will take the subject only as far as AS and others who will go on to A level. In large sixth forms, there may be separate classes in Year 12 for those intending to finish at AS and those intending to study for two years to A level. Evaluate the effect of the organisation and the extent to which teaching is adapted to reflect it.

The way the modular specifications are translated into curriculum organisation will also vary. If examinations are taken at the end of the year, topics can be taught in any order. It is for schools to decide on the organisation of their teaching and examining, and for you to evaluate its effectiveness.

Some effects of unsound organisation may be:

- the course becomes too fragmented and students do not see the links;

- the course is not cohesive, and students' work does not build well on what has gone before because teaching is not sufficiently responsive to what has been done in other parts of the course;

- progression is lost because modules are taught in an order that precludes the use of students' prior knowledge or inhibits the sequential build-up of knowledge, undertstanding and skills;

- work towards the end of the courses is disrupted because of a build-up of re-sits of module examinations.

Some courses require work placement and other off-site provision. The extent to which they contribute to courses being seamless and progressive in the way students' knowledge, understanding and skills are built up reflect effective planning and management.

Provision for key skills

How effectively does the school provide for students to develop key skills?

Where specific provision is made for key skills, schools will have different policies on how they teach and assess them. Schools might:

- provide some 'workshop' teaching to enable the weaker students to reach at least a basic minimum level;

- lay on optional courses;

- have a fully co-ordinated package for teaching and assessing key skills that extends across the curriculum.

Private study or non-taught time

Evaluate the amount of non-taught (private study) time in sixth-form students' programmes, and how well it is used. Commonly, students with the most demanding programmes of subjects and courses have little or no programmed private study time, while those with less demanding work loads have more than they need and, perhaps, more than they can effectively cope with. This can occur late in a student's sixth-form career as a result of dropping one or more subjects.

Explore issues such as the following in relation to students' learning and achievement:

- the extent to which the allocation of private study time is planned, as opposed to being what is left when the rest of the student's timetable has been pieced together;

- whether students are given any guidance or coaching in how best to plan and use their private study time;

- whether the overall balance of their time, including taught, private study and homework time, is right for them;

- whether there are adequate study facilities and resources.

Enrichment studies and activities

Does the school provide enrichment through its curricular and extra-curricular provision?

Evaluate the full range and quality of activities that extend beyond the academic and vocational subjects and courses. 'Enrichment' programmes vary significantly from school to school. Normally, they will encompass sport and recreational activities, studies contributing to spiritual, moral, social and cultural understanding including PSHE, citizenship and careers education and the statutory provision of religious education. Part of the enrichment programme may be used to focus on key skills. Take account of how well the programme responds to students of particular backgrounds, such as overseas students and refugees.

Where activities are not part of the formal curriculum, it may be that the timetable or other arrangements allow for only a proportion of students to be involved. Consider whether students have the opportunity to participate. The extent to which they are actually and positively involved reflects their attitudes to the sixth form and what it has to offer.

In many sixth forms, students have the opportunity and are encouraged to be involved in the management of the sixth form and the wider life of the school through, for example, a sixth-form council or groups responsible for organising social, cultural and other activities. These can make significant contributions to students' personal development.

Shared provision of sixth-form courses

Does the school effectively integrate any multi-site provision to give a coherent programme of learning?

Schools faced with the problems of a small sixth form may have consortium or partnership arrangements with other schools or colleges. This widens the choice for students. Whilst recognising the difficulties that schools can encounter in managing multi-site provision, assess the effectiveness of the arrangements to ensure that students get the best possible benefits.

Consider:

- the effect on students' work patterns;

- the impact of the time students and/or teachers spend commuting between sites;

- the arrangements for monitoring the performance and progress of students on different sites;

- the effect of the location of provision on subject and course choices;

- students' access to suitable resources;

- whether equality of opportunity is assured

- the extent to which the school is aware of the quality of provision, particularly teaching and learning, in partner schools, and the steps taken when it falls short of what the 'home' school seeks;

- access to enrichment activities;

- the impact on 'main school' timetabling.

The School Inspections Act 1996 as amended by the Education Act 1997 (Schedule 6) gives inspectors right of entry to schools other than the one being inspected, if those schools make a significant contribution to the provision for some of its students. Observing and evaluating work with other institutions will need to be carefully and sensitively planned and managed. Guidance on this is included in Part 3 of the *Supplement*.

5. *How well does the school care for its students?*

Inspectors must evaluate and report on:

☐ the effectiveness of the school's assessment and monitoring of students' academic performance, and reporting of students' progress to those who need to know;

☐ the effectiveness of the school's educational and personal support and guidance, including:

- the information, advice and guidance to students in relation to their studies, considering guidance onto and through courses, and their career progression;

- support on personal issues;

☐ the steps taken to ensure students' health and safety.

In determining their judgements, inspectors should consider the extent to which the school:

- has effective arrangements for assessing students' attainments and progress;

- uses its assessment information to guide its planning;

- has assessment, verification and moderation procedures which follow awarding body requirements;

- reports assessments clearly and regularly to students and those with an interest, such as parents;

- provides effective support and advice for all its students, informed by the monitoring of their academic progress, personal development, and attendance;

- makes induction arrangements that help students settle effectively into post-16 work;

- ensures that students receive impartial guidance that is effective in leading them towards courses, study or career opportunities appropriate for them;

- accurately diagnoses individual learning needs and ensures that students receive effective additional support throughout their studies;

- ensures the health and safety of students.

Sixth form inspection focus

Effective assessment, support and advice are crucial in helping students to derive full benefit from the sixth form, and the evaluation of them should have a strong place in sixth-form inspection.

The thoroughness and suitability of assessment underpin effective diagnosis of students' learning needs and any additional support they need, the tracking of their progress, and identification of what they need to do to extend their learning. In addition, the assessment of assignments contributes to accreditation in many courses; reliability and accuracy are essential.

Students have a succession of important decisions to make that affect their future as they enter and move through the sixth form. The advice, guidance and support to help them to make the right decisions are heavy responsibilities on the school. In addition, students will often look to the school for support on personal matters.

Aspects of care such as welfare, health and safety continue to be important, but it is unlikely that inspection of these will need to be extensive. Check how well students' welfare is assured and the working environment is safe, particularly for disabled students. On some courses, students will be working in specialist facilities for which there may be particular health and safety requirements. You are not a health and safety inspector, but you should not let pass any health and safety concerns that become apparent to you. Report these to the headteacher and the governing body, and keep a record of having done so.

Making judgements

Evaluate the suitability and thoroughness of the assessment of students' achievement and progress. Look at students' work, particularly assessed work, records and reports.

In talking with students, find out whether they have an accurate picture of how well they are doing. Check if they are aware of the steps they need to take to improve, what and how targets are set, based on assessment, and whether they are helped to evaluate their achievement. Judge the quality and frequency of reporting to students and their parents.

Take account of the additional criteria in the modified *Schedule* when evaluating the information, advice and guidance for students. In the main school, careers guidance is normally evaluated and reported in the context of the curriculum; in the sixth form, include it with your evaluation of support and guidance.

Ensure that the following aspects of advice, support and guidance are pursued:

- advice and guidance before students embark on courses;

- monitoring and support during their programmes, including advice about specialisation as students move from Year 12 to 13;

- guidance into higher education, further education, training or employment.

Follow up comments about advice, support and guidance in students' questionnaire responses by talking with a representative sample of students. Assess how successfully the guidance and support has worked out for them.

Sample tutorial sessions. Some might be group sessions geared towards a general tutorial programme; other might be occasions for individual students to meet with their tutors.

Determine the quality and suitability of care, support and guidance for students such as those who have special educational needs, those for whom English is an additional language and those who are gifted or talented. Consider, too, whether there is consistency in the quality of guidance for students following academic and work-related courses. Are all students supported in a way that ensures that they have equal opportunities and access to courses? Are any groups left unsupported or with unsuitable advice or guidance?

The following characteristics illustrate where to pitch judgements about the quality of care and support for students.

	Assessment	Advice, support and guidance
Very good or better	Assessment is regular, rigorous and supportive. The assessment of each significant piece of work leads to an opportunity for the teacher to raise matters with students, and for students to clarify the assessment. Students are given accurate information about their achievement, are helped to understand the strengths and weaknesses in their work and assessment is used to set targets. Reporting is accurate and diagnostic and gives a clear picture of students' performance.	Regular, recorded contact between students and their tutors allows progress to be reviewed and action agreed. Tutors know students very well, and ensure help is available as they need it. They get expert and timely advice and support on higher education applications. Support for students whose results fall below expectations is thorough and sensitive. Careers guidance is of high quality. Information before students start courses is clear and backed by careful, impartial advice. Students are comfortable that support is always sensitive to their needs when personal problems arise.
Satisfactory or better	Regular assessments of work provide students with information about how well they are doing and how to improve. Targets are set.	Sound and detailed records are kept, and tutors use these as the basis of regular discussions with students about their progress and any difficulties. Careers guidance is sound, and students have ready access to careers advisers and a good range of up-to-date literature. Students get clear information about course options, and inappropriate choices are discussed with them. Support is available if personal problems arise.

Features likely to indicate that assessment is unsatisfactory:

- assessments are insufficiently thorough and regular, and do not enable students to form an accurate picture of their achievement;

- not enough is done to enable students to develop the skills and knowledge to enable them to evaluate their own work systematically;

- there are no arrangements for monitoring the overall workload and achievement of students across the range of their courses or subjects.

Features likely to indicate that support and guidance are unsatisfactory include:

- students are given insufficient help or inappropriate advice when signing up for courses, such that courses are poorly matched to their needs, capabilities and aspirations;

- students receive insufficient help and advice to enable them to develop a realistic strategy for their applications for higher education;

- students get into serious difficulties with their work before members of staff become aware of it to the point that ineffective action is taken;

- students are unsupported or poorly advised if personal problems arise;

- any group of students is denied equality of opportunity or access to courses or employment through poor advice, support or guidance;

- students' health and safety and freedom from oppressive behaviour are not assured.

Reporting Requirements

Report on how the school cares for its students as follows:

Report section	Full inspections	Short inspections
5. How well does the school care for its students?	Use a subheading **'sixth form'**, but under this separately report on **'assessment'** and **'advice, support and guidance'**.	Include a section **'How well does the school care for its students?'** in Part D of the report. Include subheadings **'assessment'** and **'advice, support and guidance'**.
	Where there are health and safety concerns relating to the students' work environment that require reporting, they should be associated with 'accommodation' in the section on 'Leadership and Management'. Other issues relating to welfare should be included with 'advice, support and guidance'.	

☐ **Effectiveness of the assessment and monitoring of students' performance and progress**

Does the school have suitable and effective arrangements for assessing students' attainments and progress? Does it use assessment information to guide planning? Does the school accurately diagnose individual learning needs and ensure effective additional support?

Students should understand the criteria that are used to evaluate their work and how these relate to the course assessment objectives. Aspects of assessment to focus on are:

- **accuracy and reliability** of the picture it gives to students of how they are doing.

  The accuracy and reliability of assessment depend on teachers' sound knowledge and understanding of the subjects or courses, and the course and assessment objectives.

  Look for a balance of enough information for students so that they have a realistic assessment of their prospects and support where they are experiencing doubts. Encouragement should be objective so that it does not arouse false and unachievable expectations. Students need regular assessment as they move through the relatively short post-16 courses.

  Courses usually have prescribed assessment procedures. It is not your task to police whether teachers are following the awarding body's procedures to the letter. However, you must evaluate whether students are being assessed in a way that gives them a fair and complete picture of their achievements in relation to the course objectives. Report if students' prospects are jeopardised by the school's misunderstanding of the assessment requirements. Explore how verifiers' reports for vocational courses are used.

- **clarity of the messages,** so that students know what they have done well and what they need to do to improve.

  Cross-reference evidence from three sources:

  - scrutiny of the teacher's written comments on the students' work;

  - oral comments when work is returned to students;

  - students' views of the extent to which assessment is helpful to them.

- **action that results** from assessment.

  Early assessment is necessary to identify any additional needs that students have. In some cases these may be general across the teaching group, while in others they may be individual. Accurate diagnosis of individual learning needs is essential if students are to receive effective additional support. Track through the action taken and its effect.

  Assessment through a course should lead to action by students and teachers. The readiness of students to pursue matters raised through assessment reflects on their attitudes to work. Be alert to ways in which teachers follow up particular difficulties, whether through help to individual students or re-focusing the teaching to a group as a whole. Assessment may lead to re-shaping the course programme, for example where it identifies weaknesses that could be overcome by teaching modules in a different order.

- how effectively assessment strengthens **students' ability to evaluate their own achievements accurately** and recognise what they need to do to improve.

- the quality and helpfulness of **records and written reports** about students' achievements.

  Although parents continue to have a vested interest in students' performance, clear and regular summary records and reports for students themselves can be of particular value.

☐ Advice, support and guidance for students

Does the school provide effective support and advice for all its students, informed by monitoring? Do students receive impartial advice that is effective in guiding them towards courses, study or career opportunities appropriate for them?

Effective advice, support and guidance are necessary for students:

- before they join the sixth form, to ensure that they are taking up the right courses or programmes for them and have a realistic chance of success;

- in the early stages of their time in the sixth form when some students re-negotiate their course programmes. It is not uncommon for them to modify initial decisions as they see how they are working out in practice;

- during their courses, to ensure that they keep on track with their work as they should, and any personal difficulties are dealt with;

- as they prepare to leave school, to ensure they are properly advised and supported in their applications to university or employment.

Evaluate how well students are guided onto courses by looking at the information they are provided with, and by talking with them about their experiences before they joined the sixth form. Often, they will have attended 'open evenings' and personal interviews. The quality of this guidance can affect how well students get on with their courses. Analysis of course retention rates should prompt questions about the quality of guidance. Assess whether the advice to students is fair and balanced, by exploring, for example, whether options other than continuing at school were considered. Continuing at school may not be the best option for some students.

Tutorial support for students, however it is organised, is part of the school's care in the sixth form. At best, tutorial arrangements provide:

- an overview of how individual students are coping with their work, and contribute to setting and putting in place strategies for continued improvement;

- early warning of difficulties, that are dealt with before they grow;

- a means through which students are able to raise, in confidence, any concerns or worries that arise they have as result of the work programme or other personal circumstances;

- continuity of support throughout the course, so that students are known well.

In the best of practice, progress is regularly reviewed, points for action agreed and tutors and students work together to ensure that additional help and other support are available. Meetings will often result in a written note of the main points being shared and subsequently reviewed.

Where the school is involved in formal consortium arrangements, or where individual courses are followed at other schools, track how well assessment and other information is shared between schools. The consistency and quality of monitoring, support and guidance should not be jeopardised by students attending more than one school or college.

Continuity of tutorial contact throughout the sixth form enables tutors to provide sound guidance and support on higher education and employment applications. This is supplemented by specialist advice when needed. The quality of written information and guidance about, for example, UCAS applications, contributes to students knowing that they are well supported.

Evaluate the quality of the school's advice, support and guidance arrangements by looking at information, records, observing tutorial and other similar sessions, and by discussion with students and teachers, particularly tutors and key staff in the sixth form. Where the student's questionnaire is used or the school has gathered students' views in other ways, use this evidence.

Induction

Do the school's induction arrangements help students settle effectively into post-16 work?

The transition from Key Stage 4 to post-compulsory education can bring difficulties for students. These include:

- settling into different patterns of work;
- 're-starting' after GCSE examinations;
- responding to timetables that give students more control over their time in school;
- facing different levels of work;
- more intensive study of fewer subjects or courses, and often new subjects.

Arrangements to help students overcome such potential difficulties vary. They include:

- induction courses at the end of the previous or start of the new term;
- enhanced tutorial sessions at the start of the year;
- specific induction courses on, for example, study skills.

Arrangements within subject areas will often complement arrangements that apply across the whole sixth form. Evaluate their coherence and how effectively they help students settle into their work with confidence and a feeling of support.

In subjects that continue from Key Stage 4, look at how the progression into the new work is managed. This includes how well the school identifies and remedies gaps in knowledge, understanding and skills for moving to advanced level work. Those who have some prior learning in the subject should not have to mark time while others, new to it, catch up.

Careers guidance

Do students receive impartial advice that is effective in guiding them towards courses, study or career opportunities appropriate for them?

In the sixth form, the quality of careers guidance should be evaluated alongside other forms of support and guidance.

Students should have easy access to well-informed guidance from suitably qualified and experienced advisers, as well as to up-to-date reference materials, including higher education information, and Internet sources. Increasingly, many students will have access to personal advisers through the Connexions strategy.

Work-related education includes the contribution of school/business partnerships, work experience programmes and the use made of the school's contacts with universities and colleges. In addition, an integral part of AVCE and GNVQ courses may be work placement. The coherence of the provision is included in the evaluation of 'How good are the curricular and other opportunities offered to students?', but these links with work also impinge on guidance, teaching and other aspects of the school.

6. How well does the school work in partnership with parents?

Inspectors must evaluate and report on:

☐ parents' and students' views of the school.

In determining their judgements, inspectors should consider the extent to which:

- parents are satisfied with what the school provides and achieves;

- students are satisfied with the sixth-form provision.

Sixth-form inspection focus

In the sixth form, parents should and will contribute their views of the school, but students' views become equally important as they take greater responsibility for their lives. Although adults at home contribute to decisions, students themselves will have considered their options for post-16 education. They will have weighed up whether to stay at the school or go elsewhere. As a result, their views about how the school is meeting their needs have particular significance.

Making judgements

The mechanisms for gaining parents' views are well established. If you are the registered inspector ensure that you draw out from the parents' meeting any views about the sixth form.

The school may choose to use the student's questionnaire. Use your analysis of responses and any other surveys to form initial views about how far students are satisfied with the sixth form, and to identify issues to follow up. You may also be able to form impressions about students' views from the preliminary visit to the school.

 The following characteristics illustrate where to pitch judgements about the parents' and students' satisfaction with the sixth form.

Very good or excellent	Parents and students express very strong, positive views about the school, supported by sound reasons for choosing it for post-16 provision. They have a clear understanding of what the school aims to do and how it goes about its work. Students' approval for the school is reflected in their involvement in school life, their work and their willingness to help to enrich the sixth-form ethos.
Satisfactory or better	Parents and students are generally supportive of the school and what it achieves. Students are involved in activities and recognise the benefits they gain from life in the sixth form. Parents and students have no major concerns about the sixth form.

Features likely to indicate that parents or students are dissatisfied with the sixth form include:

- students are apathetic towards sixth-form activities;

- students show little sense of determination or of belonging;

- parents or students are concerned about standards, the quality of education or leadership and management;

- parents and students feel that consultation and communication are weak.

Reporting requirements

Report on the views of parents and students about the sixth form as follows:

Report section	Full inspections	Short inspections
6. How well does the school work in partnership with parents?	This section does not need a 'sixth form' subheading. Report and evaluate students' views in relevant sections of the report.	Reference to students' and parents' views should permeate relevant sections of the report.

The RCJ includes a **new grade on students' views. This is included in section 2.2** to be consistent with the JRF used in college inspections.

Guidance on using the criteria

☐ Students' views of the school

Are parents and students satisfied with what the school provides and achieves?

Ascertain parents' views through the parents' meeting and the questionnaire. Tease out issues that specifically relate to the sixth form and test them as you would issues in the main school. Do parents feel as well informed about the sixth form and how well it is providing for their children as they do about the main school? It will be helpful to set parents' views alongside students' views.

Responses to the student's questionnaire will give insights into the views of a wide cross-section of students. However extensive the responses on paper, talk with as many students as you can. Follow up issues, and explore what students value about the sixth form, what makes them feel good about it, and how they feel about the school's capacity to meet their needs. Home in on whether individual students feel they are getting the best possible deal. Involve managers and other staff as well students in following through issues, and look for direct evidence in tutorial sessions, meetings, activities, minutes and so on.

Evaluate how effectively the school works with its students, and how responsive it is to their concerns by tracking how particular issues have been dealt with. Many schools have sixth-form councils. They give insights, for example, into students' views and priorities, and also clues about relationships, the level of responsibility they are given, their willingness to initiate and take on responsibility, and how concerns are resolved.

Evaluate students' comments about the sixth form against what you see of their attitudes to sixth-form life and work, their involvement with activities, and sense of being at ease in the school whilst being clear about their purpose in being there.

7. How well is the school led and managed?

Inspectors must evaluate and report on:

☐ how effectively the sixth form is led and managed within the context of the whole school, promoting high standards and effective teaching and learning;

☐ how well the governing body fulfils its statutory responsibilities and accounts for the performance of the sixth form and influences its work;

☐ how effectively the school monitors and evaluates the performance of its sixth form, diagnoses its strengths and weaknesses and takes effective action to secure improvements;

☐ the extent to which the school makes the best strategic use of its resources in the sixth form, linking decisions on spending to educational priorities within the school as a whole;

☐ the extent to which the principles of best value are applied in relation to the school's sixth-form work, ensuring that it is cost-effective;

☐ the adequacy of staffing, accommodation and learning resources, highlighting strengths and weaknesses in different subjects and areas of the curriculum where they affect the quality of education provided and the educational standards achieved in the sixth form.

In determining their judgements, inspectors should consider the extent to which:

- leadership ensures clear direction for the work and development of the sixth form, and promotes high standards;

- the school has explicit aims and values for its sixth-form work, including a commitment to good relationships and equality of opportunity for all, which are reflected in all its work;

- there is rigorous monitoring, evaluation and development of teaching;

- the school identifies appropriate priorities and targets, takes the necessary action, and reviews progress towards them;

- there is a shared commitment to improvement and the capacity to succeed;

- governors fulfil their statutory duties in helping to shape the direction of the sixth form and have a good understanding of its strengths and weaknesses;

- educational priorities are supported through careful financial management;

- good delegation ensures the effective contribution of staff with management responsibilities;

- the number, qualifications and experiences of teachers and support staff match the demands of the curriculum;

- the accommodation allows the curriculum to be taught effectively;

- learning resources, including specialist equipment, are adequate for sixth-form courses;

- there is effective induction of staff new to the school and the school is, or has the potential to be, an effective provider of initial teacher training;

- the best value principles of comparison, challenge, consultation and competition are applied in managing the sixth form to ensure cost-effectiveness.

Sixth-form inspection focus

The leadership and management of the sixth form and of the school as a whole are closely bound together. Consider how the leadership and management of the school affects the sixth form, and look at the effectiveness of any specific management arrangements for it. Judge on the basis of what works, rather than a preferred model.

There could be potential conflicts between what is good for the school as a whole and what is good for the sixth-form students. If so, determine whether they are recognised by senior management and governors, and how they are resolved. Establish how far the governors help to shape the direction of the sixth form, and judge their awareness of its strengths and weaknesses in developing it further.

Assessing the effectiveness of leadership and management as it affects the sixth form includes looking at how provision shared across sixth forms is handled. Here, the planning and practicability of the arrangements are crucial. Evaluate where the balance lies between the benefits to students and any disadvantages.

Focus on the extent to which leadership creates an effective and improving sixth form, in which all students can and do achieve and are well supported. Assess whether the sixth form is inclusive in all it does.

A judgement about the cost-effectiveness of the sixth form must be made. Part of this involves evaluating its costs and how resources are allocated. The distribution of spending between the main school and the sixth form reflect management decisions in the school as a whole. New funding arrangements are being introduced from 2002. Funding for the sixth form will come from the LSC via the LEA.

A summative judgement about the effectiveness of leadership and management as it affects the sixth form is required.

Making judgements

The characteristics of effective leadership and management in the sixth form are similar to those for the school as a whole. But there are features that are distinctive relating to the rationale for the provision the school makes in the sixth form, how it responds to local circumstances and how any joint provision is managed. Evaluate the steps taken to ensure that the sixth form is cost-effective, including the school's monitoring and evaluation of its performance post-16. Where there are joint arrangements with other schools or colleges you may need to contact senior staff in partner schools to discuss their views of the effectiveness of these arrangements.

The summative judgement about leadership and management should give greatest weight to how effectively they promote high standards and effective teaching and learning, including how well performance in the sixth form is monitored and evaluated and steps taken to secure improvements.

The following characteristics illustrate where to pitch judgements about the effectiveness of leadership and management in the sixth form.

Very good or better	The rationale for provision in the sixth form is clear and sensible, and a set of values underpins its work. The relationship between the sixth form and main school – the features and benefits which each is expected to derive from the relationship – is clear. There are challenging targets for achievement, progression and retention that are commonly understood, and likely to be achieved. Quality assurance through monitoring, evaluation and improvement is effective in ensuring very good teaching so that students are achieving as much as they can. The governors take an active role in quality assurance and set clear priorities for the development and operation of the sixth form. Financial resources and staff are effectively deployed to achieve educational priorities, without detriment to any sections of the school. Where the sixth form operates in partnership with other institutions, responsibilities for leadership and management and for the day-to-day operation of the partnership are clearly identified and work effectively.
Satisfactory or better	Management of the sixth form is sound, and a good development plan has been prepared based on a clear view of the relationship between sixth form and main school to ensure at least satisfactory achievement. Senior managers and governors have a sound overview of the strengths and weakness of the sixth form, and these are reflected in the development plan. Resources are sensibly deployed such that the effectiveness of parts of the school is not jeopardised. Courses and subjects are staffed by teachers with appropriate experience and qualifications and less experienced teachers are effectively supported. Consortium arrangements are satisfactorily managed.

Features likely to indicate unsatisfactory leadership and management as it affects the sixth form include:

- a significant amount of unsatisfactory sixth-form teaching;

- standards in the sixth form are significantly lower than they should be, or standards achieved by particular groups of students are unjustifiably low in comparison with others;

- quality assurance practices in the sixth form are inadequate;

- financial planning is weak, with no convincing rationale for the distribution of resources between the main school and the sixth form;

- absence of a clear rationale for the sixth form or of its relationship with the main school;

- no account is taken of other provision for post-16 education in the locality, and students are discouraged from considering alternatives;

- consortium arrangements are poorly supported or managed by the school.

Reporting requirements

Report on leadership and management in the sixth form as follows:

Report section	Full inspections	Short inspections
7. How well is the school led and managed?	Use a subheading '**sixth form**', but under this, separately report on '**leadership and management**' and '**resources**'.	Include a section '**How well is the sixth form led and managed?**' in Part D of the report. Include subheadings '**Leadership and Management**' and '**Resources**'.
	The section on resources should focus on the adequacy of staffing, accommodation and learning resources, but should draw from the section on teaching any significant matters relating to the use of resources.	

Include the overall judgement about the effectiveness of leadership and management as they affect the sixth form in the sixth-form annex to the summary report.

Guidance on using the criteria

The guidance on using the evaluation criteria for leadership and management in the *Handbook for Inspecting Secondary Schools*, pages 90–98, and *Evaluating Educational Inclusion*, pages 27–32, can also be applied separately to management and leadership in the sixth form.

☐ Leadership and direction in the sixth form

Does leadership ensure clear direction for the work and development of the sixth form? Does the school have clear aims and values for its sixth-form work? Do governors fulfil their duties in helping to shape the direction of the sixth form?

As part of the evaluation of the school's aims and objectives, establish how far there is a clear rationale for the sixth form, and what specific aims and objectives there are for its operation and development. Identify any particular benefits that the headteacher, governors and senior managers consider important in the link between the main school and sixth form. Evaluate how well these perceptions are shared by the staff, students and parents and whether they are achieved in reality.

☐ **Monitoring, evaluation and action to secure improvement**

Is there rigorous monitoring, evaluation and development of teaching?

Procedures should be in place for the sixth form as for the school as a whole. Where there is effective monitoring, evaluation and improvement of teaching in the main school, check that they apply or have been effectively adapted to the sixth form. It is critical that teachers are at the cutting edge of their subjects and have up-to-date expertise in the courses they teach. Assess how well the school ensures and develops this further.

Look for evidence of the school critically evaluating what is achieved and analysing the reasons, particularly by exploring the effectiveness of teaching. For example, does the school follow up value-added analyses that show students in particular subjects, or groups, are not doing as well as they can? How effective are middle and senior managers in turning round subject teaching which is not good enough?

Targets and expectations

Does the school identify appropriate priorities and targets for retention, achievement and employment?

Currently, schools are not required to set specific performance targets for the sixth form, but evaluate whether expectations are sufficiently high for all groups of students, and whether there is a commitment to improve. Assess how effectively performance information is used to challenge what is achieved, and to set targets. However they are expressed, the sixth form should have a suitably challenging range of improvement objectives towards which all staff are working. Assess whether targets for the sixth form are backed up by an effective improvement plan to achieve them.

☐ **Strategic use of resources**

Are educational priorities supported through careful financial management? Are the best-value principles of comparison, challenge, consultation and competition applied in managing the sixth form to ensure cost-effectiveness?

New funding arrangements will be in place from 2002, and these will need to be taken into account in evaluating how effectively resources are deployed. In the meantime, funding is within the context of the whole school and remains much as it has been.

The school should have a clear rationale and sound justification for the spending decisions it takes in relation to the sixth form and individual courses.

Establish whether the sixth form is living within its means as opposed to being subsidised from the main school or *vice versa*. There need not be an absolute match between the income and expenditure for the main school and sixth form, but an analysis of the costs of main-school and sixth-form provision gives you the basis for hypotheses and issues to pursue. A school should be able to explain why it has decided to put on particular courses that are perhaps being subsidised by others. Evaluate the influence of other local provision and shared sixth-form arrangements. It should not be an automatic judgement that courses that recruit very small numbers of students indicate unwise decisions. Above all, evaluate the effect of spending decisions without any preconception about ideal provision.

Further details on the analysis of costs between main school and the sixth form are in annex D. Guidance on evaluating cost-effectiveness is included in section 1, 'What sort of school is it?', earlier in this part of the *Supplement*.

Consider the extent to which the principles of best value – comparison, challenge, consultation and competition – are applied in relation to the sixth form. The guidance in the *Handbook for Inspecting Secondary Schools*, page 97, applies equally to the whole school and to the sixth form.

Consortium and partnership arrangements

An additional set of management issues has to be considered in these circumstances. Timetabling to achieve maximum benefit for students from the partnership without putting additional strain on them and on staff is a key factor. Examine how effectively problems such as potential loss of time in travelling and timetable clashes are resolved. For students who spend a considerable proportion of the week on a site other than their official 'base', arrangements for tutorial contact and for domestic matters such as storage facilities should be considered. The essential question to ask is whether these arrangements provide a good deal for the students at reasonable cost to the school.

☐ **Adequacy of staffing and other resources**

Do the number, qualifications and experience of teachers and support staff match the demands of the curriculum? Does the accommodation allow the curriculum to be taught adequately? Are learning resources adequate for sixth-form courses?

The teaching of A-level and vocational courses requires teachers with good qualifications and scholarship in their subjects and expertise and experience in the relevant vocational areas. Use the student/teacher ratio for the sixth form and individual subjects as an overall measure of quantitative adequacy, but also explore the match of qualification to subjects and courses taught. Set any questions that arise against the effectiveness of work seen in the classroom.

Where some of the teaching for the sixth form is provided by other institutions, judgements about the adequacy and suitability of staffing should include these teachers.

For many courses, specialist resources and facilities are necessary. They include materials to set courses in a vocational context and specialist apparatus and equipment in science and technology subjects and courses. Do not engage in an audit of equipment as an exercise itself, but, in seeking to explain why achievement is as it is, be alert to gaps in provision or particularly positive features of resourcing that are having an impact on teaching and students' achievement.

Students' capacity to research, to compete assignments, and to extend their knowledge beyond the work covered in class depends on the availability of up-to-date reference texts, easy access to ICT, and adequate study facilitates. Schools may direct students towards specialist reference sources and other similar facilities outside school. There will be circumstances where the facilities are adequate but little is done to encourage their use or teach the skills to use them. Base your evaluations of resources, or the lack of them, on the impact that they have.

10. The standards and quality of teaching in curriculum areas, subjects and courses in the sixth form

Full and Short Inspections – Part E of the inspection report

The following evaluation requirements apply to subjects or courses that are inspected and reported in detail. Where work is sampled across the sixth-form provision, the evaluation elements enclosed in a box are not required.

Inspectors must evaluate and report on:

☐ the range of provision and take-up of subjects and courses;

☐ performance data, including the retention of students on courses;

☐ the standards of work seen, highlighting what students do well and could do better;

☐ how well students achieve;

☐ the quality of teaching, highlighting effective and ineffective teaching in the subject and relating the demands made by teachers to students' learning and the progress they make;

☐ any other aspects of the quality of education that have a bearing on what is achieved in individual subjects and courses, including subject or course planning, resources, assessment or support and guidance;

☐ leadership and management in the subject, especially the extent to which management of the subject or course is directed towards monitoring, evaluation and improving performance;

☐ the overall quality of provision in the subjects or courses inspected, and the main strengths and areas for improvement.

The requirements for inspecting subjects and courses are set out in Part 2 of this *Supplement*.

The quality of teaching and learning, and the success of students in subjects and courses, lie at the heart of a successful sixth form. The ethos of sixth forms is almost invariably good. Cut through this and ask whether students are achieving as well as they can and whether teaching and learning are good enough to ensure that students gain the most they can from their time in the sixth form. The inspection of subjects and courses in the sixth form must have a critical edge.

Making judgements

Use the relevant booklets in the series *Inspecting Subjects and Courses Post-16* alongside the more general guidance in this *Supplement* and *Evaluating Educational Inclusion*.

- **Start by interpreting performance data** and, with any other evidence you have, form pre-inspection hypotheses about standards and provision in the subjects you are inspecting.

- During inspection, see how far the results from previous cohorts of students are mirrored in the **standards of current work**. Use your observations to identify what students are doing well and what they could be doing better. Where the standards you see are different from those indicated by previous results you must explain how and why. To form a view about standards use evidence from: your observations in class; analysis of students' work; talking with students, testing what they know and understand; as well as looking at assessment and other records.

- **Rigorously test whether all students are achieving as well as they can**. Use value-added indicators as fully as possible, and compare performance in different subjects. In your discussions with students, find out how far they can respond to challenge by asking them questions which test the limits of their knowledge and understanding. Set this assessment against what is expected in their day-to-day work.

- Ensure that your **judgements about provision, particularly teaching, and leadership and management** are firmly **rooted in the impact they have**. A judgement that teaching is good yet achievement is no better than satisfactory needs a convincing explanation.

As important as direct observation is, judgements about teaching and learning draw on evidence from more than just lessons. Judgements are not based on averaging lesson grades, especially where few lessons are seen. Use all the evidence you have to form a professional judgement. Distinguish between the occasional weak or just satisfactory lesson, and more systematic weaknesses in a subject area that result in students getting a less than satisfactory deal.

The **strengths and areas for improvement** identified must focus on the most important things, that is standards and achievement and the factors that most affect them.

The summative judgement about the quality of provision

The summative judgement about the quality of provision in a subject or course should reflect the overall **effectiveness** of work in the subject. Provision cannot be satisfactory if, overall, students are not achieving well enough. This would be the case where there is any significant underachievement by particular groups of students. Your judgement about teaching and learning should reflect students' achievement. Use this judgement together with that for achievement as a starting-point for your overall judgement; they have the greatest weighting. Moderate your judgement, if necessary, by considering other factors that have a **significant** impact on what is achieved. These could include:

- the characteristics of particular cohorts of students;

- significant changes of staffing that have been beneficial or otherwise;

- shared sixth-form arrangements;

- the support and guidance for students;

- provision of learning resources.

Reporting requirements

Report on subjects and courses as follows:

Report section	Full and short inspections
Part E: Subjects and courses in the sixth form.	Both full and short inspection reports have a part on sixth-form subjects and courses. The components are:
	- a table showing the performance data for all subjects and courses in the sixth form;
	- curriculum-area reports with sections on individual subjects and courses where they are inspected in detail and brief comments on other work seen;
	- a bullet pointed set of 'strengths' and 'areas for improvement', and an overall evaluation of the quality of provision, for each subject or course inspected in detail.
	Subjects or courses that are taught at different levels, for example, AVCE in Art and Design and the equivalent Intermediate GNVQ course are reported under the one subject or course title.
	Further guidance on reporting is included in Part 6 of this *Supplement*.

Part 5

Inadequate Sixth Forms

Towards the end of an inspection, the team must consider formally whether or not the school has an 'inadequate sixth form', except in those cases where the team has concluded that the school as whole requires special measures. Essentially, the team should ask the questions:

- is the school failing or likely to fail to give pupils over compulsory age an acceptable standard of education? or

- does it have significant weaknesses in one or more areas of its activities for pupils over compulsory school age?

If the team agrees 'Yes' to either question, the registered inspector must report that in her/his opinion the school has an inadequate sixth form. It is subject to HMCI's agreement in a similar way to schools requiring special measures.

Relationship between special measures, serious weaknesses and an inadequate sixth form

The judgement about the inadequacy of a sixth form is **separate** from whether the school as a whole requires special measures, has serious weaknesses, or is underachieving. But a view about the adequacy of provision in the sixth form will contribute to these other judgements.

The key relationships to bear in mind are as follows.

- If the school is found to require special measures, this is an important judgement about the school as a whole. Where weaknesses in the sixth form contribute to this judgement, this will be clear in the report, **but a formal judgement about the adequacy of the sixth form is not required;**

- An inadequate sixth form may be the main or one of a number of reasons for a school having serious weaknesses. However, it is not automatic that a school with an inadequate sixth form has serious weaknesses as set out in the School Standards and Framework Act 1998. For example, in a large school with a very small sixth form, the sixth form might be judged inadequate without the school requiring special measures or being judged to have serious weaknesses. Where a school is deemed to have serious weaknesses **and** an inadequate sixth form, both judgements need to be clearly made.

Judging that a school's sixth form is inadequate

The pre-inspection analysis and interpretation of performance data and other information may suggest particular weaknesses. These must feature in the pre-inspection commentary as matters to explore.

Towards the end of the inspection you should review the evidence and, as a team, judge whether or not the sixth form is adequate.

Sixth forms vary significantly in size, in their aims and purposes, and their context; some are part of consortium arrangements. These contribute to making the judgement complex. Some small sixth forms in rural or deprived areas set out to provide continuing education, probably through just one-year courses, for students who might otherwise not find alternative post-16 education or training. Other sixth forms may be large, providing mainly academic A-level courses.

As a team you should consider the context carefully, but should not shirk from the judgement that the sixth form is inadequate where the evidence clearly points to it.

Ask yourselves how well the school is doing for the post-16 students it has. Some questions are set out in the box.

Are students achieving as well as they can in the subjects or courses studied?

– as part of this consider the progress they make; it is helpful here to consider a range of indicators including: value added from the end of Key Stage 4; the value added from Key Stage 3; individual student profiles that may indicate that performance is consistently low in some subjects, or for some particular groups of students, compared with others.

Do most students continue on the courses they enrol for, accepting some changes of course during a period of 'settling in'?

– normally 'retention' in school sixth forms is high; no national data are available yet, but you should note cases where retention falls below 75–80%. However, take care in interpreting data where take-up numbers are low.

Do students attend regularly?

Is the teaching good enough across the range of subjects?

– where teaching is satisfactory or better in less that 90% of lessons overall, this should signal concern. But care is needed in interpreting lesson statistics where relatively few lessons are seen. You must make professional judgements about the quality of teaching overall and in individual subjects.

Does the school give adequate guidance to students when they are recruited so that the subjects and courses that they take match their needs, interests and aspirations?

Do students receive adequate support through their courses so that they know how well they are doing and are helped to improve?

How well is the sixth-form provision achieving the school's aims and objectives for these students?

Do leadership and management have a beneficial effect on the sixth form?

Is the sixth form cost-effective?

You must decide whether the school:

• is failing to provide adequately for its students; or

• has significant weaknesses in one or more areas of its activity for its sixth-form students.

For the purposes of the second category, 'areas of activity' can be regarded as 'teaching', 'achievement'; 'support and guidance' or 'leadership and management' as they affect the sixth form. Equally, it could relate to provision in individual subjects where significant numbers of students are involved.

An inadequate sixth form that is failing or likely to fail to provide an acceptable standard of education

Here, it is likely that significant numbers of students or particular groups of students are not getting an acceptable standard of education across several key subjects. A combination of weaknesses, for example unsatisfactory teaching and achievement with perhaps less than adequate support and guidance, may be contributing to this.

If your answers to a significant number of the questions above are 'no' or 'not enough', it could indicate that the standard of education is inadequate.

Significant weaknesses in one or more areas of the school's activity

Here there may be fewer weaknesses but they are general across the sixth form, or significant numbers of students are getting a poor deal across a few subjects. Normally, if any of the areas indicated above are unsatisfactory or worse, it is likely to lead to a judgement that the sixth form has significant weaknesses and is, therefore, inadequate. Unsatisfactory provision or achievement in a single subject, unless it affects many students should not normally lead to a judgement that the sixth form has significant weaknesses.

Completing the Record of Corporate Judgements

Where an inspection team is of the opinion that the school has an inadequate sixth form, this must be recorded in the RCJ with the reasons. A distinction must be made between the two categories of inadequacy.

Procedures to be followed

When a sixth form is judged to be inadequate, the procedures mirror those for schools judged to require special measures in the *Handbook for Inspecting Secondary Schools,* page 158. These include:

- informing the School Improvement Division in OFSTED (tel: 020 7421 6594);

- making the headteacher aware of the team's thinking before the registered inspector leaves the school;

- explaining that the report may be delayed;

- completing and sending Form X (included with Update 36) to OFSTED;

- submitting to the School Improvement Division a draft of the report together with the RCJ and other evidence such as inspectors' Notebooks particularly relating to the sixth form.

What happens next?

The procedures for corroboration mirror those set out in the *Handbook for Inspecting Secondary Schools,* page 159, for schools judged to require special measures.

The School Improvement Division will consider the evidence and, usually, visit the school before recommending to HMCI whether or not to agree that the school has an inadequate sixth form.

Reporting

Where a sixth form is found to be inadequate, and HMCI agrees, this should be made clear in the summary report **and** the sixth-form annex. The following wording should be included underneath the box relating to 'Areas for improvement':

'I am of the opinion, and HMCI agrees, that the school has an inadequate sixth form in terms of paragraph 1(2) of Schedule 7 of the Learning and Skills Act because **either** it is failing to give pupils over compulsory school age an acceptable standard of education **or** it has significant weaknesses in … for pupils over compulsory school age.'

Amendments can be made, as with special measures judgements, when HMCI does not agree or when the judgement is 'likely to fail'.

The weaknesses leading to the judgement should be clearly stated and not clouded by other, less significant, issues.

Cases where the school overall requires special measures, has serious weaknesses or is underachieving

If the school is judged to require special measures, whether or not weaknesses in the sixth form contribute to that judgement, there should be no formal statement about the adequacy of the sixth form. The form of words relating to special measures in the *Handbook for Inspecting Secondary Schools*, page 159, should be used.

If the school has serious weaknesses, or is underachieving, and it has an inadequate sixth form, both judgements should be reported. For example:

'The school has serious weaknesses. I am also of the opinion, and HMCI agrees, that the school has an inadequate sixth form … [wording as above].'

The fact that the school has serious weaknesses or is underachieving need not appear in the sixth-form annex unless the serious weakness(es) is (are) in the sixth form.

Publication of the report

Procedures mirror those for schools judged to require special measures. In addition to sending the report to the Department for Education and Skills (DfES), you must also send a copy to the LSC.

Part 6

Report Writing

The inspection report must give a picture of the school as a whole. Changes to the report structure for schools with sixth forms are to ensure that evaluations of the sixth form are fully and distinctively reported.

A summary of the modified report structure is in Part 2 of this *Supplement*. Throughout Part 4, the 'Reporting requirements' tell you how aspects are included in the report.

Main findings and summary report

A new feature is the **sixth-form annex** to the summary.

Continue to highlight features of the school as a whole in the **main part of the summary**. For example, provision or achievement in the sixth form could still feature in 'What the school does well' and 'What could be improved'. Where this is the case, the commentary in a **short inspection** report should make brief reference to its main features, but should also refer to the separate part of a short inspection report that deals with the sixth form more fully.

The **sixth-form annex** concentrates on the effectiveness of the sixth form and standards and quality in curriculum areas in the sixth form. For an example, see below.

Reports on subjects and courses in the sixth form

The structure of this part is also new.

The part begins with a **summary of the performance data** in subjects and courses offered in the sixth form.

It then has **sections dealing with each of the curriculum areas** in which work has been sampled and/or in which subjects or courses have been inspected in detail. The curriculum areas are listed in table 5 in Part 2 of the *Supplement*.

The components of the curriculum-area sections are:

- a brief introductory section:
  - specifying what subjects or courses were inspected in detail;
  - commenting on other work seen, and any particular features of the performance data in those subjects.
- reports on the subjects inspected in detail including:
  - the strengths and areas for development in the subject;
  - a summative judgement on the quality of provision.

Subjects or courses at different levels are reported under the one subject or course title.

For an extract from a curriculum-area report, see below.

Extract from sixth form summary annex

ANNEX: THE SIXTH FORM

INFORMATION ABOUT THE SIXTH FORM

The sixth form of this large 11–18 comprehensive school has 420 students and is expanding. There is a small number of minority ethnic students, mainly Indian, who speak English well. It provides a wide range of subjects and vocational courses. Two thirds of students from year 11 continue into the sixth form, and a few students join from other schools. The 16+ examination results are well above average, and so most students embark on two-year programmes leading to A-level or the advanced vocational certificate of education (AVCE).

HOW GOOD THE SIXTH FORM IS

The sixth form is successful and cost-effective. Students learn very effectively and achieve good results. The sixth form caters well for its students through a wide range of courses, and provides a rich environment for their personal development. Teaching in the sixth form is good in most subjects and very good in psychology, sociology and design and technology. Results have been well above average for several years. The main strengths and areas that could be improved in the sixth form are:

Strengths

- students achieve good results overall, and do particularly well in sociology, physical education, design and technology, geography and mathematics;
- students are mature and confident – an impressive group of young people;
- teaching is good, with an above average proportion of lessons where it is very good or better; it is often exciting and students respond very well and make substantial gains in their learning;
- the school offers a wide range of courses, and provides rich opportunities for students' personal and social development;
- leadership and management of this large sixth form are very strong, with a focus on teaching and learning in the development planning;
- the school provides sensitive guidance and support.

What could be improved

- opportunities and encouragement for students to engage more in class discussion;
- the tutorial programme, to ensure that students gain as much benefit from it as they do from their other work;
- printed materials on careers and employment, which are dated.

The areas for improvement will form the basis of the governors' action plan. Strengths and areas for improvement in individual subjects/courses are identified in the sections on individual subjects/courses in the full report.

THE QUALITY OF PROVISION IN INDIVIDUAL CURRICULUM AREAS

The table below shows overall judgements about the provision in the subjects and courses that were inspected in the sixth form. *Judgements are based mainly on the quality of teaching and learning and how well students achieve. Not all subjects in the sixth form were inspected.*

Subject/course	Overall judgements about provision, and comment
Mathematics	**Good.** Results are above average and rising; they are better than would be expected from students' GCSE results. Course work is a particular strength. Staff have strong subject knowledge and teaching is good.
Chemistry	**Good.** Results were above average in 2000, with a little above average 'value-added' from GCSE. Students are achieving well as a result of generally good teaching, but marking is not regular or rigorous enough.
Biology	**Satisfactory**. Standards are improving as a result of better planning, and are now about average. Teaching and learning are satisfactory overall. The feedback from assessment, though, is too uneven in quality.
Design and technology	**Very good.** Standards in the A-level design and technology course are very high; teaching is consistently very good

. . . and so on for other subjects inspected, linking them where this fits the school's organisation, for example, modern languages

In other subjects, work was sampled. Teaching was at least satisfactory, but a lesson in which teaching was excellent was seen in physics and there were some very good lessons in geography. These subjects are both strong in the school.

OTHER ASPECTS OF THE SIXTH FORM

Aspect	Comment
How well students are guided and supported	Good quality support and guidance is maintained throughout Years 12 and 13. Students are well inducted into the sixth form. Information about sixth-form courses is good. Students are well informed about career options and opportunities beyond school. Students' progress is monitored very well and they are set clear and realistic targets which motivate them.
Effectiveness of the leadership and management of the sixth form	Leadership and management of the sixth form are **excellent**. Development planning is very strong and has a central focus on teaching and learning. Performance of all groups of students is carefully analysed and evaluated and effective steps taken to overcome weaknesses. The governing body plays a very effective part in the leadership of the sixth form.

STUDENTS' VIEWS OF THE SIXTH FORM

What students like about the sixth form	What they feel could be improved
• Teachers know them very well and go out of their way to help them. • They are taught very well, and are expected to work hard. • The range of social activities is very wide. • Their views are listened to. • The support and help they receive with independent study.	• The programme of personal and social education taught in tutorial sessions. • The space available for independent study. • A few students felt they could be treated more like adults.

Students are very positive about the sixth form, the range of opportunities it offers them, and the guidance and support they receive. The strengths identified by students are well-founded. The facilities for independent study are good, but on occasions the centre was overcrowded and students found it difficult to work. Teaching in the tutorial sessions is not as stimulating as in most subject lessons, and the programme includes aspects that could be dealt with in subject areas, but overall the tutorials are satisfactory. The school recognises students' increasing maturity in the way the sixth form is organised and the responsibility students have.

COMPARING PROVISION IN SCHOOLS AND COLLEGES

Inspectors make judgements about provision in subjects and courses, and about leadership and management, in the range: excellent; very good; good; satisfactory; unsatisfactory; poor; very poor. Excellent and very good are equivalent to the judgement 'outstanding' in further education and sixth form college reports; poor and very poor are equivalent to 'very weak'.

SCIENCES

1. The focus was on chemistry and biology, but physics was also sampled. In physics, examination results were above average in 2000 and students did as expected considering their GCSE results. Two lessons were observed. Both were at least good. In one, excellent teaching included particularly good explanation, regular review and a well-structured sequence of activities. This led to students gaining a very secure understanding of the properties of materials.

Chemistry

Overall, the quality of provision in chemistry is **good.**

Strengths

- results showed a marked improvement this summer, and were above average;
- students have a sound grasp of concepts, apply them well in classwork and in answering routine questions, and overall are achieving well;
- teaching is good; lessons are well structured with a range of activities which effectively help students to build up their knowledge and understanding effectively;
- in small groups, students share ideas freely and work well together;
- the subject is well led and a good range of new learning resources is being built up.

Areas for improvement

- marking is not as thorough as it could be and some basic errors are being missed;
- the less capable students tend to be passive in class discussion; although well supported in other ways, they are not brought into discussion enough;
- the targets for students that stem from the monitoring of their performance are not sharply enough focused on learning goals.

2. The GCE A-level examination results this summer showed a significant improvement after some weaker years, and were above average. All students who took the examination gained a pass grade and the proportion gaining the highest grades, A and B, was a little above average. Male and female students did equally well. Very few students did not complete the course. In relation to their GCSE results, they did a little better than expected. A few students with modest GCSE results did very well.

3. The standards of work of current students are also above average. In Year 13, students are achieving well in relation to predictions based on their GCSE results. In the lessons seen, they were doing well as a result of effective teaching which demanded much of them. The lesson structure and activities clearly focused their learning. In one lesson, students drew well on their knowledge and information in books to predict successfully the products of an organic chemistry reaction and explain how and why it occurred. In another, students showed good understanding of transition metal chemistry to explain reactions. Most students recall knowledge well and apply it, but their written work does not always show the same confidence as their work in class.

4. Students in Year 12 are only a little way into their course, but are achieving much as expected. They show good knowledge and understanding of introductory organic chemistry and basic concepts such as atomic structure and bonding. Students are successfully moving on from their GCSE work into new areas. Most are tackling calculations, for example to find formulae or

concentrations of solutions, with increasing confidence. However, for a few, calculations present difficulties. There is scope, particularly among the male students, for more systematic and rigorous setting out of calculations and naming of organic compounds.

5. Teaching is good overall, and students learn well as a result. The principal features of teaching are clear objectives, sharp planning, brisk pace, and a range of methods and approaches to bring about learning. Teachers show good subject knowledge in their questioning and explanations and in the tasks they set. The lesson on transition metal chemistry in Year 13, for example, included a demonstration to focus on reactions that needed explanation, opportunities for students to work individually and together to check their learning and formulate new ideas, short experiments to test predictions, and effective explanation and drawing together of ideas by the teacher. Students responded confidently to the changes of activity. Of the five lessons seen, two were not as dynamic, and, although sound overall, did not result in such secure learning.

6. Much of the written work demanded of students takes the form of structured questions which follow up lessons. Day-to-day marking has improved through the year, but some sets of questions remain unchecked by the teacher or students. In some cases, simple errors, for example in nomenclature, are uncorrected. This is an area for improvement in the context of teaching that has many strong features.

7. Students learn well. They are attentive, work productively and respond well to the supportive teaching and different learning styles that they experience. They rose to the challenge of predicting possible products and developing explanations for an organic chemistry reaction in Year 13. In lessons, time is used well. Students support and help each other effectively and, in groups, talk and listen to each other maturely as part of their learning. They are not always as confident in offering ideas in more open discussion, and the less capable are not always brought into question and answer dialogues as much as they could be.

8. The independent work students undertake in the sixth-form learning centre is very well prepared, and tasks complement the content of lessons well. Students are confident in using books and ICT. They approach this work maturely, and most are able to extract information and make their own notes on, for example, the evolution of models of the atom. A few are less confident in seeing the focus of tasks where explanations are needed.

9. The good teaching and learning result from work in the subject being well led and managed. There is a commitment to building on what has already been achieved and to improving standards. A new scheme of work effectively reflects the subject requirements, and sets the stage for good teaching. It identifies a range of approaches to encourage effective learning. A good range of helpful learning support materials is being developed. Target-setting, based on careful analysis of students' performance in tests, is becoming well established, although targets are not yet sharply enough focused on specific learning goals.

Biology

etc.

Annexes

These annexes will be revised to reflect, for example, changes in published data for 2001 examinations and new funding arrangements for sixth forms. The student's questionnaire may also change.

New versions of the annexes will be available on OFSTED's website.

Annex A

Student's Questionnaire

A copy of the questionnaire is included at the end of annex A. The annex also includes notes that you may find helpful to share with schools.

Protocol for using the student's questionnaire

The following protocol must be observed.

- The school should be invited to use the questionnaire, but the decision to use the questionnaire is in the hands of the school and its governing body, and completion of it is voluntary for students.

- Where the school decides to use the questionnaire, sufficient copies should be made available, together with envelopes for responses, for each student to be offered a copy.

- The registered inspector should agree with the school the arrangements for ensuring the confidentiality of students' responses.

- Arrangements for distributing the questionnaires and briefing students might be discussed with the school, but this is a matter for the school.

- The registered inspector or contractor should analyse students' responses; although schools may offer, the registered inspector or the contractor must do it.

- Arrangements should be made with the school for completed questionnaires, in their sealed envelopes, to be sent to or collected by the registered inspector before the inspection; this could be along with parents' questionnaire returns.

- Issues arising from the analysis of questionnaire returns should be shared with the school as soon as possible, and included in the pre-inspection commentary, but each student's response should remain confidential and not shown to the school.

- Concerns or particularly positive features raised by students must be followed up during the inspection and evaluated.

- The analysis of responses will not be included in the inspection report, but a digest of students' views from the questionnaire and other sources of evidence, together with inspectors evaluation of them, will be included in the sixth-form annex to the summary report.

Student's questionnaire: information for schools and governing bodies

Gauging parents' satisfaction with the quality of education provided by a school through seeking their views is an established part of inspection.

Students in the sixth form have an increasing stake in their education and how well it prepares them for moving on to employment, training or higher education. Their views of the sixth form are as important as those of parents or carers.

During the inspection, inspectors will talk with students about their work and life in the sixth form. The school may also have evidence about students' views, for example, through surveys. The sixth-form annex to the summary report will include a digest of students' views and inspectors' evaluation of them.

Your registered inspector will invite you to use a questionnaire that OFSTED has developed as a means of gaining students' views before the inspection. **Its use by the school and completion by students is voluntary.**

Where it is used:

- the views of individual students will be confidential to the inspection team, but any significant general issues, including particularly positive features or concerns, will be shared with the school;

- the inspection team will follow up any issues that emerge;

- the inspection report **will not** include a tabulated analysis of students' responses.

If, as a school, you choose to use the questionnaire, the registered inspector will provide you with sufficient copies and envelopes for each student to be offered a questionnaire.

The school should:

- distribute the questionnaires at the same time as the parents' questionnaire (if it is used), and set a similar return date;

- explain to students:

    - the purpose and significance of the questionnaire;

    - the importance of students thoughtfully considering their responses as individuals;

    - the arrangements to ensure the confidentiality of responses, including the use of sealed envelopes;

    - that their involvement in the survey, and the inclusion of their name on the questionnaire, are voluntary.

- provide a means for students to return their questionnaires in confidence; this might involve a 'post-box' in a secure place;

- agree with the registered inspector how the responses in their sealed envelopes will be returned to him or her for analysis before inspection.

Your registered inspector will discuss the use of the questionnaire and the arrangements with you.

Student's Questionnaire

OFFICE FOR STANDARDS
IN EDUCATION

Name of school being inspected

This questionnaire is for you, as a student, to give **your** views about the sixth form if you wish. Its completion is voluntary. Your response will be **confidential to the inspection team**. No staff in the school will see your comments, but the inspection report will refer to the views of students generally.

For the statements below, please tick the box that best corresponds with your views about the sixth form.

	Strongly agree	Tend to agree	Tend to disagree	Strongly disagree	Don't know
1 The choice of courses allows me to follow a programme suited to my talents and career aspirations	☐	☐	☐	☐	☐
2 The printed information about subjects and courses in the sixth form was clear, accurate, and helpful	☐	☐	☐	☐	☐
3 I was given helpful and constructive advice on what I should do in the sixth form	☐	☐	☐	☐	☐
4 The school helped me to settle well into the sixth form and sixth-form work	☐	☐	☐	☐	☐
5 I am taught well and challenged to do my best in all or almost all of my subjects or courses	☐	☐	☐	☐	☐
6 I am helped and encouraged to study and research topics independently	☐	☐	☐	☐	☐
7 My work is thoroughly assessed, so that I can see how to improve it	☐	☐	☐	☐	☐
8 I am kept well informed about my progress in relation to the qualifications I hope to get	☐	☐	☐	☐	☐
9 Teachers are accessible to help me if I have difficulties with my work	☐	☐	☐	☐	☐
10 I am well-advised by the school and/or careers advisers on what I should do after I leave school	☐	☐	☐	☐	☐
11 I could rely on strong and sensitive support and help from the school if I had personal problems	☐	☐	☐	☐	☐
12 Outside my main subjects, the school provides a good range of worthwhile activities and enrichment courses	☐	☐	☐	☐	☐
13 I feel I am treated as a responsible young adult in the school	☐	☐	☐	☐	☐
14 The school listens and responds to the views of its sixth-form students	☐	☐	☐	☐	☐
15 I enjoy being in the sixth form and would advise other students to join the sixth form in this school	☐	☐	☐	☐	☐

You can comment further on these or other things, particularly strengths or areas where you would like to see the sixth form improve, by using the back of this questionnaire or a separate sheet. Please do not refer to individual teachers.

Thank you for filling in this questionnaire. Please seal it in an envelope for the inspector leading the inspection. Your school will tell you about the arrangements.

Name (optional)　　　　　　　　　Year Group (12/13)　　　　Date

Annex B

Analysis and interpretation of data on standards

This annex concerns the interpretation of data typically included in PICSI and, now, sixth-form PANDA reports. These reports are being continually developed and will over time include new sets of information. The guidance here should be taken as indicative of the types of analysis and interpretation that you should do.

Getting to grips with the data about standards is an essential pre-inspection activity. Central hypotheses about the sixth form are rooted in their analysis and interpretation.

Whole-school summary results

PICSI and PANDA reports typically include an analysis of the school's results in A-level courses over recent years, comparing them with national averages. Tables B.1 and B.2 allow you to compare the school's data for the latest year with national averages for schools of the same type.

Table B.1. PICSI data for a mixed comprehensive school

GCE A/A Level/Advanced GNVQ Average Point Score	1996	1997	1998	1999	2000	1998/00
Candidates entered for less than two GCE A Levels or AS equivalent						
School – Number of candidates	4	9	15	13	10	38
School – Average points score for each candidate	0.3	1.6	2.0	1.2	2.0	1.7
England – Average points score for each candidate	2.7	2.7	2.8	2.8	2.7	2.8
School difference	-2.4	-1.1	-0.8	-1.6	-0.7	-1.1
Candidates entered for two or more GCE A Levels or AS equivalent						
School – Number of candidates	58	66	69	66	74	209
School – Average points score for each candidate	12.4	9.9	14.8	11.2	12.2	12.8
England – Average points score for each candidate	16.8	17.1	17.6	17.9	18.2	17.9
School difference	-4.4	-7.2	-2.8	-6.7	-6.0	-5.1
All candidates entered for Advanced GNVQs						
School – Number of candidates				13	12	
School – Average points score for each candidate				9.2	7.5	
England – Average points score for each candidate				10.2	10.6	
School difference				-1.0	-3.1	

Other Vocational Qualifications 2000 (Candidates aged 16–18)	Intermediate Level	BTEC National	IB Diploma
Number of candidates entered in school	14	n/a	0
Percentage of candidates achieving qualifications	71.4	n/a	n/a
England	73.2	n/a	76.5

Table B.2: GCE A/AS Level results by type of school (national)

	Type of school	Number of 16–18 year olds entered for less than 2 A/AS	Average point score for each candidate entered	Number of 16–18 year olds entered for 2 or more A/AS	Average point score for each candidate entered
Boys	Comprehensive	767	2.6	3,995	16.8
	Selective	572	4.2	6,439	23.6
	Modern	76	1.7	113	8.9
Girls	Comprehensive	1,101	3.1	5,050	17.0
	Selective	547	3.6	6,4230	24.2
	Modern	140	2.7	337	13.5
Mixed	Comprehensive	18,195	2.6	78,120	17.2
	Selective	528	3.4	4,456	23.4
	Modern	630	2.8	1,106	12.0
Total	Comprehensive	20,063	2.7	87,165	17.2
	Selective	1,647	3.7	17,315	23.8
	Modern	846	2.7	1,1556	12.1

Extract from pre-inspection commentary

Overall **A/AS point scores** have been **below the national average** for several years. They are also below the average for mixed comprehensive schools. The point score for students taking less than two A levels is below the national average.

For GNVQ entries, **Advanced** results are **below the national average**, but **Intermediate** results are **close to national average**.

Areas for further exploration with HT at pre-inspection visit:

- What is his explanation for the relatively low GCE A-level results? Is it well-founded and convincing?

- What is her view of/explanation of the difference between Advanced and Intermediate GNVQ pass rates?

- What are the entry requirements for different courses?

- What is the profile of the A-level students in terms of prior attainment?

- Does the school carry out value-added analyses? What are the consequences?

- Does the school analyse results by ethnicity? If not, why not?

Performance data for individual subjects

Table B.3 shows results that might typically be available on an individual subject, in this case A-level English literature. Tables B.4–7 show national comparison data. These allow you to:

- compare the school's results in your subject with the national average;

- investigate whether there is any significant difference in the attainment of male and female students;

- compare the school's results with those of similar types of school.

Table B.3. Results in English literature (example comprehensive school)

2000	No. of candidates	Grades achieved						
		A	B	C	D	E	N	U
Male	11	1	2	2	3	2	1	0
Female	17	3	4	6	3	1	0	0
Total	28	4	6	8	6	3	1	0

	2000			1999			1998		
	A–B grades %	A–E grades %	points score %	A–B grades %	A–E grades %	points score %	A–B grades %	A–E grades %	points score %
Male	27.3	90.9	4.9	33.3	88.9	5.3	50.0	100.0	6.0
Female	41.2	100.0	6.6	36.4	100.0	5.6	27.3	90.9	4.7
Total	35.7	96.4	5.9	35.0	95.0	5.5	30.8	92.3	4.9

Table B.4. GCE A-level results by subject; all maintained secondary schools – all pupils

	2000			1999		1998	
Subject	A–B grades %	A–E grades %	points score %	A–B grades %	A–E grades %	A–B grades %	A–E grades %
English Literature	36.4	95.6	5.9	35.6	94.9	35.2	94.4

Table B.5. GCE A-level results by subject; all maintained secondary schools – boys

Subject	2000			1999		1998	
	A–B grades %	A–E grades %	points score %	A–B grades %	A–E grades %	A–B grades %	A–E grades %
English Literature	37.2	94.7	5.9	36.7	93.9	34.2	93.4

Table B.6. GCE A-level results by subject; all maintained secondary schools – girls

Subject	2000			1999		1998	
	A–B grades %	A–E grades %	points score %	A–B grades %	A–E grades %	A–B grades %	A–E grades %
English Literature	36.1	96.0	5.9	35.2	95.3	35.6	94.8

Table B.7. GCE A-level results by subject; comprehensive schools – all pupils

Subject	2000			1999		1998	
	A–B grades %	A–E grades %	points score %	A–B grades %	A–E grades %	A–B grades %	A–E grades %
English Literature	33.1	95.1	5.7	32.4	94.3	32.1	93.7

Extract from pre-inspection commentary in the inspection notebook:

Overall, the A-level English literature results in 2000 were close to national average for all maintained schools, but slightly higher than for all comprehensive schools.

Results for **female** candidates are **above the national average**; results for **male** candidates are **below average**. In 1999, results were closer to the national average for both genders. In 1998, they were a little below the national average for females, while only two males took the exam in that year.

Areas for further exploration:

- Why lower results for this year's male students?

- Check on prior attainment; have sufficient gains been made?

- Any evidence of bias in teaching?

- Are there any analyses based on different ethnic groups taking English?

Avoid the trap of reading significance into the proportion of students achieving one particular grade compared with national averages. Judgements should only be made on the proportions of candidates who achieve a particular grade **or higher**.

Where small numbers of candidates are entered in particular subjects, there are dangers in comparing data on a single-year basis. Use three-year rolling averages to get a broad picture of the standards that are typically reached, but be alert to any clear trends that emerge from the data for a number of successive years.

Over the next few years more data on subjects and courses will be available in PICSI and PANDA reports. But for inspections early in the autumn term, they will always be at least one year out of date. Obtain the most recent results from the school. Where possible, these should show the numbers of candidates taking each subject and achieving each grade, separately for male and female students, for each subject over the last three years. The school may not have results for male and female students and for different ethnic groups separately or may have an incomplete set. If so, you should not ask for further analysis to be done by the school. Use what is available, and evaluate the effect of the absence of such analyses, bearing in mind the statutory responsibilities on schools.

Annex C

Analysis and interpretation of value-added data

Comparisons of raw results with national averages, whether for all schools or for schools of a particular type, provide information on attainment in the recent past. They tell you little about achievement because they do not take account of the ability or prior attainment of the students.

Little can be deduced from the national benchmark group that is used in the PICSI report for 'similar schools' comparisons for Key Stages 3 and 4 results, nor from considering the school's GCSE results, since these are based on all pupils in the main school cohort.

Schools with very different attainment at GCSE might have sixth forms with very similar potential because they apply the same criteria for entry onto advanced level courses. On the other hand, the students studying one subject might have greater potential than those studying another subject because the first subject tends to attract more students of higher ability.

To assess the progress of the students generally in the sixth form, or of those taking particular subjects, you must consider their attainment at the end of the course in relation to their attainment at the start. Progress over time contributes to the evaluation of achievement.

Find out if the school, or individual departments, have any analyses of attainment at the end compared with at the start of courses – value-added analyses. They might be analyses undertaken by the school, the subject department, or the LEA. In some cases, schools may use commercially available services for analysing results, or they may undertake their own analysis using national data available from the DfES.

The usefulness of value-added analyses depends on what the school or department compares itself against. If the school has undertaken its own analysis, it might only compare subjects with all others in the school. This gives no indication of how subjects or the sixth form as a whole rate in relation to a national picture. Similarly, an LEA scheme might only compare the sixth form with others in the same LEA. Comparisons with national data are the most useful.

Some commercial schemes include guidance on which value-added measures can be regarded as significant. In the absence of such guidance, avoid placing too much weight on data where the number of students is small, although a pattern repeated over several years would be of more significance.

Examples of value-added analyses and their interpretation are given below.

Example 1

Figure C.1. Value-added analysis for one year's A-level results

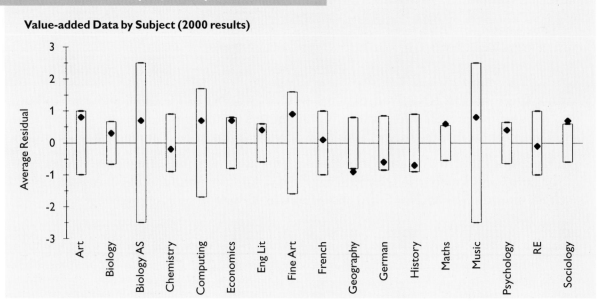

Figure C.1 is similar to the sort of diagram that might be obtained by a school from a commercial scheme. It shows, for each subject, how the school's value added compares with the national pattern. The diamonds indicate the school's performance and the rectangles indicate the ranges of results that might reasonably be expected when the cohort sizes are taken into account. It is only where the diamond lies outside the rectangle that it should be regarded as indicating significantly high or low value added. The rectangles are different sizes, partly because of national differences between the subjects but mainly because of the differences in cohort sizes in this school – in general, the larger the cohort size, the smaller the rectangle.

In this case, it is only in mathematics and sociology that the performance was significantly better than might have been expected for these students, and in geography it is poorer. The analysis suggests that achievement in mathematics and sociology is good, but in geography it is unsatisfactory.

Figure C.2. Value-added analysis for the last three years' A-level results

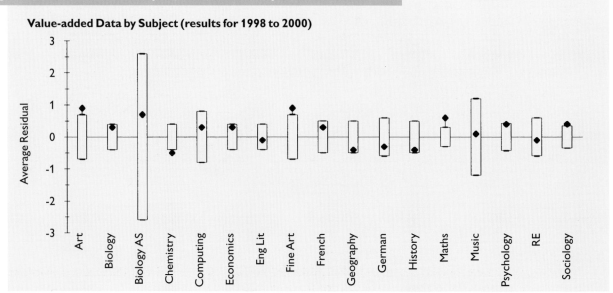

Figure C.2 shows data for the same school, but using results for the last three years. Most rectangles are smaller, because the total cohort size over the three years was bigger. There are four subjects where the analyses suggest good achievement over the last three years. Notice how art had roughly the same value-added measure in 2000 as over the three years 1998–2000. The 2000 result on its own is not sufficient to be counted as significant, but when the same pattern is repeated over three years it is enough to be significant.

Extracts from pre-inspection commentaries in inspection Notebooks:

Mathematics: Value-added analysis suggests good achievement both in 2000 and over the last three years.

Chemistry: Value-added analysis shows some under-achievement – not enough in 2000 to be counted as significant, but apparently the same pattern over the last three years which *is* enough to be significant.

Schools which do not use a commercial value-added scheme may use data and graphs from the DfES to do their own value added analysis. An annual statistical bulletin[8] from the DfES (for example, *Statistical Bulletin 02/01*, published in March 2001) contains a number of graphs showing the national picture. By plotting their own results on these graphs a school can see how well it is doing, in value added terms, in comparison with national averages. The next two examples illustrate this. The lines show the national picture, the points show how well each of the school's students achieved. A point above the upper median line shows a student who had good value added; a point below the lower median line shows poor value added.

Example 2

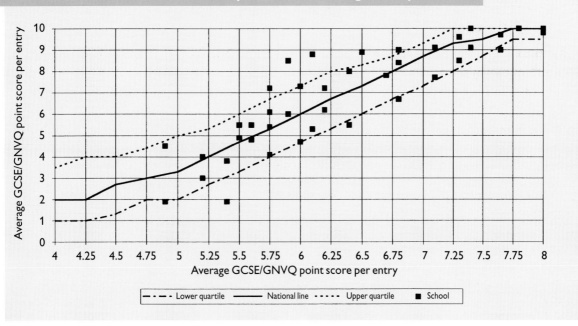

Figure C.3. The school's GCE A/AS results compared with the average GCSE points score

---

8   Available on the Internet at **www.dfes.gov.uk/statistics** (follow the link for value added). The statistical bulletin also contains tables which explain all the points scores which are used.

Look at the graph in figure C.3. Here the points are fairly evenly distributed on either side of the median line. There is a slight tendency for points to be above the median rather than below it. Also, points tend to be higher above the upper quartile line than below the lower quartile line, but this tendency is probably not sufficiently great to be able to describe the achievement as better than satisfactory.

Example 3

Look at the graph in figure C.4. Here, the points are distributed above and below the line, but an important feature is seen when students of different prior attainment are considered. In the left hand half of the graph – the part which shows those students who had lower attainment when they started in the sixth form – the points are well distributed above and below the median line. This indicates satisfactory achievement. But in the right hand half of the graph, there are far more points below the median line than above it, and there are far more points below the lower quartile line than there are above the upper quartile line. These students appear to have been underachieving. The graph shows that although the school is achieving satisfactory value added for its lower ability students, it is not doing well enough with those of higher ability.

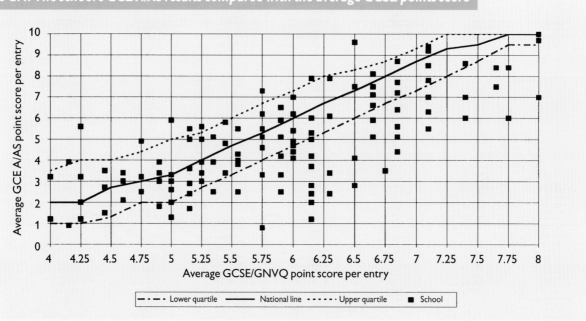

Figure C.4. The school's GCE A/AS results compared with the average GCSE points score

Extract from a school pre-inspection commentary:

Value-added analysis for 2000 indicates satisfactory achievement for lower-ability A-level students but underachievement for those of higher ability.

Initial hypotheses and areas for further exploration

Hypothesis: Teaching does not stretch the more able A-level students.

- Is the school aware of this pattern? If not, why not? If so, what has it done?

- Has there been a similar picture in previous years?

- Any evidence of differential achievement for different groups? Males/females? Different ethnic groups?

- Are expectations and challenge high enough for the more able students?

The DfES statistical bulletin also contains graphs for individual A-level subjects which the school can use to analyse value added by each A-level course separately.

If value-added analyses are not available from the school (or if none are available which will give useful information) then you can undertake your own analysis. If the school is able to provide the average GCSE point scores and the A-level results for each individual A-level student in their most recent cohort it will not take very long to plot the school's results on a copy of the DfES graph, or to do this for individual subjects. Using different colours for the two genders will help you to see if there is any difference in achievement between male and female students. Similarly, you could investigate the achievement of other groups of students.

If the school is not able to provide you with the data you need you should not ask them to collate or calculate the data specially for you. It would be possible for a member of the inspection team to do this from the school's raw examination results. It is time-consuming, but there will be circumstances where it is worthwhile. Examples might be where there are no other indicators of value added, and you suspect that particularly able students, despite gaining high A-level results, are not achieving as well as they could, or low A-level results may nonetheless represent good achievement for a weak cohort of students.

Annex D

Cost of the sixth-form provision

Note: This guidance uses concepts that are part of the current funding arrangements for sixth forms. New funding arrangements involving the LSC come into effect from 2002.

Contributory evidence about the efficiency of the sixth-form provision comes from an analysis of its costs, and in particular how they relate to the school's income overall. A spreadsheet is available to help you with this calculation.[9]

To assess the costs of the sixth form in relation to the rest of the school, two proportions must be compared:

- the proportion of the school's income which it receives in respect of its sixth-form students; and

- the proportion of its resources which are actually devoted to the sixth form.

To make the calculation of each proportion manageable, simplifications can be made:

- expenditure is considered only as the number of teacher periods devoted to lessons for the different year groups, since the great majority of a school's expenditure is on teachers' salaries; and

- for income, only the funds based on Age Weighted Pupil Units (AWPUs) is considered, since the great majority of a school's income is from this source.

Although these mean that the relative costs are approximate, they provide a sufficiently reasonable basis for hypotheses to be set up and issues to pursue in most cases. Nonetheless, take account of any significant additional funds that might be ear-marked for post-16 work such as Single Regeneration Budget (SRB) funding to pump-prime the introduction of vocational courses or funds to promote increased participation in post-16 courses.

The data for inclusion into the spreadsheet are contained in Form S2 completed before the inspection by the school. They are:

- the number of periods in the timetable cycle   (Section E13);

- the total teaching staff in full-time equivalents   (Form E2 at the end of Form S2);

- the age-weighted pupil units (AWPU) for each year group   (Section F9);

- the number of pupils in each year group   (Sections E13 and D6);

- the number of teaching periods for each year group   (Section E13).

The spreadsheet performs the necessary calculations and creates a statistical diagram to enable you to compare the two proportions.

---

[9]   Available on the Internet at **ftp://ftp.open.gov.uk/pub/docs/ofsted/ofsted.htm**

Figure D.1

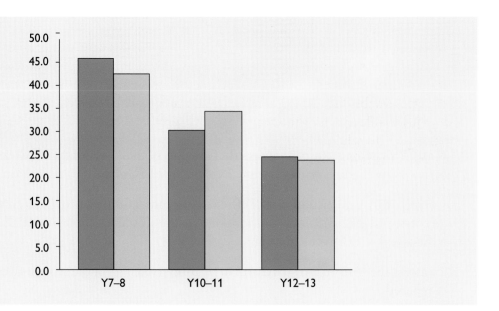

The graphs show three pairs of bars, a pair for each of KS3, KS4 and the sixth form. The left-hand bar of each pair shows the proportion of staffing resource used – an approximation for the expenditure on that key stage. The right-hand bar shows the income received in respect of students in that key stage.

In figure D.1, the income and expenditure for the sixth form are closely balanced. In figure D.2, more is spent on staffing the sixth form than is warranted by the income. In this case the main school, in particular Key Stage 4, is subsidising the sixth form. This prompts questions about the effect this is having on the quality of education in Key Stage 4, as well as whether the sixth form is being operated efficiently. These are matters to pursue with the school.

The imbalance might well be justified. In the inspection you should explore the strategic thinking behind the decisions, and evaluate their effect.

Figure D.2

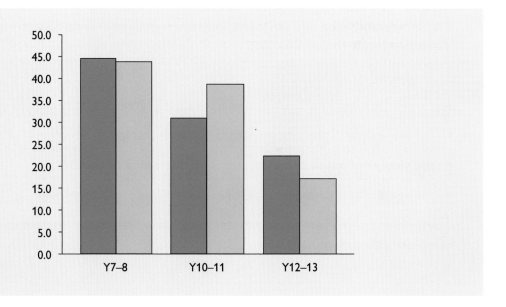

It would be important in the situation in figure D.2 to find out whether it is an unusual one for the school. It may be for one year. It might be unreasonable for a school to radically change the nature of its provision simply because one year group had fewer sixth-form students and so had made the sixth form less economic. An alternative scenario might be that the school is just developing a new sixth form and some subsidy is seen as a sensible investment in the future. The school may have decided to subsidise GNVQ courses in their first year. On the other hand, it might be claimed that it was justifiable to subsidise a sixth form because of the beneficial effect that the sixth form has on the rest of the school; that could be too simplistic a justification, particularly if the decline in sixth form numbers is a continuing trend.

Figure D.3

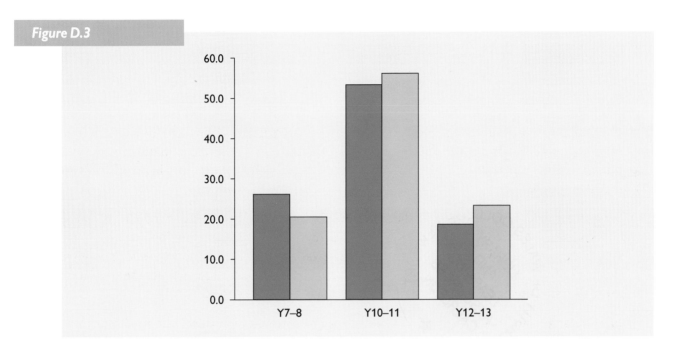

The situation in figure D.3 raises different questions. Here, the sixth form is subsidising the rest of the school. It is tempting to feel that the school is being particularly efficient, but on the other hand it may be that here the sixth-form students are not getting a good enough deal. Their taught time may be too limited for the courses they are following, and they may be expected to spend an unreasonable amount of time in private study. There may be some classes that are too large. The examination of the pre-inspection data raises questions that need to be answered during the inspection itself.

Whenever you find an imbalance investigate whether the senior management team and governors are aware of it. If they are not, then that would seem to have a significant message about financial management. If they are (or when they are), can they justify it, and do the outcomes support the justification?